Thrive and Shine!

HOW TO FIND HAPPINESS WHEN LIFE FALLS APART

Michele Joy

Soulrise Publishing
Castle Rock, Colorado

Soulrise Publishing
5139 LeDuc Court
Castle Rock, CO 80108

Editing and book design/production by Barbara Hughes

Thrive and Shine!
How to Find Happiness When Life Falls Apart/Michele Joy
1st ed.
ISBN-13: 978-0-692-12352-2

I dedicate this book to all of my patients who have taught me the true meaning of life and have given me the courage to be me, no matter what.

Contents

Ego says, "Once everything falls into place, I'll feel peace."
Spirit says, "Find your peace, and then
everything will fall into place."

– MARIANNE WILLIAMSON

Acknowledgments

Most great feats are accomplished with the help of others—not in isolation—and my writing this book is no different. I have been blessed by the love in my life. Without all of the support I've gotten on this journey, none of this would have been possible. I can't thank my mom enough for being my rock. You have always believed in me and supported me through all of my ups and downs. You've encouraged me when I was down and celebrated all of my triumphant times, no matter how small. My dad has also given me the gift of unconditional praise and he too has encouraged me to speak my truth and let my light shine.

I would like to thank my editor, Barbara Hughes, for helping to make this dream come true and for making this book better than I could have expected. I am grateful for my students and coaching clients who trusted me and allowed me to offer them love and advice. The rewards you have all given me have been great.

I want to thank my patients, both in the hospital and in hospice. I feel so lucky to have cared for you and your family members. You have all taught me the true meaning of life and how to courageously move forward in the face of adversity. The love you've given me will always be why I do what I do.

I'm grateful for my sweet boys who have provided me more love than I thought was ever possible. They teach me every day that the most important time is now, and that my happiness is the greatest gift I could give them.

Lastly, I would like to thank my sweet soul mate, Paul, who I met toward the end of writing this book. His unconditional love and support for me has helped me reach levels I didn't know I could reach. I am so blessed that I have found true love. And having him in my life reflects how far I have come. Thank you, sweetie.

Introduction

> *Believe in yourself and all that you are. Know that there is something inside of you that is greater than any obstacle.*
>
> Christian D. Larson

I was once at a local bar when my friend Krystal ran over to me, urgently telling me that she met a woman who could use my help. Being a nurse, I thought this poor woman may have been hurt and needed my medical assistance. But given that my friend was also a nurse, I was confused as to why she needed me. All Krystal told me was that if there was anyone who could help, it was me. As I approached this woman, I sensed the anger in her voice and the sadness in her eyes. She was having a heated conversation with another sad fellow, and looked at me with apprehension when I told her I was there to help.

With my friend's brief introduction of "my friend can help you," I realized that this woman did in fact need my help. But she didn't know it yet. You see, she was stuck in her unhappiness, and what my dear friend wanted me to do was give her hope; to help her see that life is not all doom and gloom and that there is meaning to the suffering.

So many of us go through life feeling like we were given the short end of the stick. We feel like suffering is par for the course and happiness is something that only lucky people feel. We also believe that happiness comes from outside of ourselves, not within. We think that if we could only find the right partner, or right career, we would be happy.

Yet, the truth is we are born happy, and that is our natural state. We come into this world with all of the power to make our lives blissful. Unfortunately, very few live out their lives in this state. We live in a world where war, poverty, and sadness are blasted into our senses. We think the poor are getting poorer; the number of people on antidepressants is at an all-time high; people are getting sicker; the rich are getting greedier.

It's no wonder many lose hope and feel like this life we are living is a kind of hell on earth. As a hospice nurse, I have seen how terribly sad life can be and how quickly lives can be taken. Yet, I have learned that life can be far richer and more beautiful if we only knew how to achieve it. If only someone could give us a pill or a magic potion that would take all the pain away and make us happy, without needing anything in return.

The truth is I have found that magic potion. I have opened up a door that leads to a life of true joy. I have danced in the morning air and breathed in a truth that holds the formula of eternal bliss. I committed to a journey that has led me down a path that was far better than I could have imagined. I am here to tell you that you can be happy. I mean really happy. But you must stop looking outside for the winning ticket. You, my friend, are it. *You* are your solution. *You* are your salvation. *You* are the magic pill. The question is: how do you access this beautiful part of yourself?

I recently listened to a teleseminar with Neale Donald Walsch, the author of *Conversations With God*, in which he revealed the answers to all of life's problems. He shared that almost everyone is unhappy because they have forgotten who they really are. They have forgotten that they are divine beings and have the power to change worlds. They live through the ego and put their spirit on the back burner. In fact, the biggest problem for humanity, according to Walsch, is that we forget that we are spiritual beings living a human experience, not the other way around.

I have come to realize in my own journey that my happiness is the core of who I am. But I had to go through some steps to get here. I had to let go of how I was doing things, and begin again. I had to start to build a foundation that would hold me, instead of standing on my tiptoes, at risk of being knocked over.

Look at the trees. They spend a good amount of their energy preparing to grow. The Chinese Bamboo spends the first four years underground; then, on the fifth year, it grows nearly ninety feet in only five weeks. This quick growth is attributed to the foundation that it had been building for all of those years.

Humans are not that different. Most of our work is internal. When our foundation is wobbly, it's often because we don't want to take the time to work on it. Many of us skip this important step because we are impatient and want quick results. We are afraid of being alone, so we jump into unhealthy relationships. We are afraid of our darkness, so we run away and pray that the mental boogeyman won't catch us. The way to stop these games is to simply stop playing. We need to take the time to go underground and start rebuilding.

Many of us go through life reacting to what is going on around us. We put others ahead of ourselves, thinking we are being noble, and than feel alone when everyone goes away. We compare ourselves to others' successes, but then don't even know what we want or what success looks like for us. We are always reaching, wishing, wanting, but we still feel empty when the things we want are achieved. Think about the rich and the famous and you will know what I'm talking about. Some of them seem to have everything and yet are miserable. They are addicted to drugs or alcohol, getting divorces at high rates, and end up in trouble with the law. Yet, by our social standards, they should be happy, right?

When things go bad, many of us latch onto something to keep us standing, be it a relationship or an addiction. We project our issues onto our next "victim" and then expect them to make us happy. It's this constant game that can go on for a lifetime, but will have dire consequences if gone untreated.

I don't say this to scare you or make you feel like there is no hope. I only share this with you so you can see that something must change. If you picked up this book, I am guessing that you are tired of living life the way you are. You are fed up with not being happy and finding yourself in unhealthy relationships. You are frustrated with having low energy and constant waves of despair or dread. You are tired of living someone else's life and want to have your own voice be heard. And most importantly, you are tired of falling down all the time and realize this yo-yo life is just not for you anymore.

The change you are looking for is you. Or rather, remembering who you *really* are. There is a diamond within you that is the most beautiful part of you. Who you are is enough, but for many, connecting with our truest self is like hiking up Mount Everest. Yet it is there, waiting to be seen again. This shining diamond is what you are looking for and once found, it will change your life.

When I became a Certified Soul Coach®, I found out that my shine, or truest self, had always been there. As I went through my training to become a Certified Happiness Coach, I began to understand the complexities around joy and why so few of us are reaching this state that is available for us to claim. I have spent the last several years teaching the Law of Attraction and have met countless souls who are all trying to find what their shine is and be truly happy. And the common issue for all of them was they didn't know where to begin. They needed a roadmap to help show them the way.

In this book I will walk you through the steps that I took that have led me to a life of true joy. I will show you ways to connect with your shine so you will never go through the dark again. I have built a foundation that is now so firm that nothing can knock me down. I started out my journey with very little hope. Yet looking back, I can see what a joy this process has been. I am excited to share these tools that I have used that have forever changed my life and will forever change your life, too.

This book is divided into three sections. Section One, *Self Awareness*, is about getting real and getting deep. It is in this section where we will break down some of those barriers that keep your truth from shining free. This is the part where you dig in the dirt and prepare a space for your seeds of life. This first step is essential and necessary in order to begin a life of true happiness. Even if you're not a gardener, you know how important it is to have good soil for your seeds. Without the right foundation, anything placed on top of it will topple over. That is why this is the first step and one that must be done.

Section Two is called *Prepare to Shift*. After laying the foundation, it is now time to start designing your plans to shine. It is here that you will be planting and watering your seeds. This section is a resource to help you see that you are not alone and that there is a divine power that is helping every step of the way. It is also here that you'll build the much-needed strength to keep going. This journey was not meant to be taken alone; and once you connect with the powerful divine helpers that are eager to assist, you will never feel alone again.

Section Three, *Steps to Transformation*, is a step-by-step process that will lead you to true, deep, and permanent transformation. This is where your tree of greatness begins to grow. You'll learn what to do once the growth really starts taking off. It's all about forward movement and how to keep a positive attitude when faced with change. When we grow into our true selves, the amount of growth can be exponential. I'm here to show you how to go through this powerful process more effectively.

I will be giving you tools that changed my life when they were given to me. I have also taught these steps to hundreds of people with great results through my Soul Coaching and Happiness Coaching programs. I have taught over 2,000 people for several years through my Law of Attraction groups where I have become an expert at using the power of the mind. These life-changing tools have not only brought me more happiness and internal joy, but they have led me along a path I had not expected to be on. My hope is that this happens for you, too.

After each chapter I offer you exercises that will help solidify what you are learning, so that this book becomes more of a lived experience than a sit-down read. Doing the work is what is going to truly change you. I also offer free guided meditations on my website to help you along the way.

I want you to do one thing and one thing only. Take this journey with me with an open mind and a full heart. Dig deep into your most sacred parts and sit there a while. I promise that when you take this journey, you *will* connect with your light and, as a result, be happier. You will start to believe in your greatness, and your shine will beam out for the world to see.

Life is meant to be magical, my friend. It's supposed to be fun! It's supposed to be joyful! You, and you alone, are responsible for this journey. *Nobody* can tell you that you can't do it. I believe in you. Each and every one of you has something special within. You were born into this life with a purpose. Once that is realized, nothing will stop you from achieving it. One of the most powerful quotes by Napoleon Hill, famed author of *Think and Grow Rich*, states, "Somewhere in your make-up there lies sleeping, the seed of achievement, which if aroused and put into action would carry you to heights, such as you may never have hoped to attain."

You have a gift that the world is waiting for. I'm so happy you are ready to take this next step in your life and finally be the person you were meant to be. The world is ready for you. The question is, are you?

Section One

Self Awareness

CHAPTER 1

Reality Check

He who knows others is wise. He who knows himself is enlightened.

Lao Tzu

My life began when I was thirty-five years old. I had been living a lie for so long, I could have quite frankly won Oscars for my brilliant performance. I wore every costume possible and plastered perfect smiles on my oh, so obedient face. I would mold myself quite easily into whatever was asked of me. I was a good listener, caretaker, mom, wife, and daughter. I bowed down to all requests and pocketed my shame and sadness in a locked-up chest that even Houdini couldn't escape. I was a con artist to my own psyche, and an accommodator extraordinaire. To put it bluntly, I was a shell of a person; completely unaware of who I was.

The lowest point came one night when I was riding my bike on a date night out with my husband. As we rode across a bridge, I seriously considered sharply turning the handlebars and ending my life. Unfortunately, this was not a new idea, since I had contemplated this dire thought before. But this time I was taken aback by how hopeless and sad I had become. In fact the only thing that kept me from flying over the edge was my two beautiful boys. I knew I couldn't leave them.

The question now was whether I could leave my marriage, which was the reason for my desperate state of mind. But since I had spent the last sixteen years of my life being molded by my husband's strength, I felt that I couldn't live with him and I couldn't live without him. So I did what I had always done. I lived in denial land.

So many of us have found ourselves in this dreaded territory. All too often we live our lives by hiding our truth in order to survive. We keep up with the Joneses simply because it's easier. We go to college, get married, and have kids. We work jobs that may not be satisfactory but we're happy they at least pay the bills.

Then we find ourselves sick, depressed, addicted, or just plain checked out. We eat more junk food. We watch more mindless TV. We go to jobs we hate. We surround ourselves with people who hurt us. Then we go to bed dreading the sunrise, since it will inevitably be another day just like yesterday. Our focus is on surviving, not thriving. In fact, many of us have sold ourselves so short we truly believe that great things don't and won't ever happen to us. We resign ourselves to the "fact" that our lives will be mediocre at best; we tell ourselves that to want anything more is ludicrous.

This lack of internal happiness has been something I have seen time and time again with my patients. For many, it wasn't until they were faced with the possibility of death that they finally questioned their life choices. Some got a second chance and started to live life with a sense of purpose. But they needed to receive a critical diagnosis to slap them in the face to wake up.

Most of us are asleep. We often walk through our days not paying attention to where we are going, and then wonder how we got there. Think about the last time you drove your car. Do you remember the route you took and what happened along the way?

For me, my life of denial was my slow suicide. It was like getting Alzheimer's and expecting someone else to show me how to get to the bathroom. I may be exaggerating a bit, but looking back, this lack of awareness was not living. It was slowly dying. And when I looked into many of my patients' faces, I knew something in my life had to change.

I once had a patient who was diagnosed with cancer and needed frequent blood transfusions to stay alive. There was no cure for her cancer, and she was given days or weeks to live. The saddest part of this was that her husband had finally retired and had just bought an RV so they could finally travel the country and enjoy life. You see, she spent her whole life supporting him and his journey, raising their children, and waiting around to finally have fun. Then when the time finally came, it was too late. I'll never forget the sadness in her eyes that said, "It's too late." And for her, it was.

I have been blessed by my years as a nurse. My patients have taught me a lot about living, simply because many of them haven't lived fully. So very often I have heard stories of shame and sadness. Most have developed insomnia and chronic pain as a result of tragedies that happened when they were children or very early in their lives. I have heard stories so sad and heartbreaking that it's no wonder such poor health has manifested in the lives of these people.

Many of my patients talk to me about their tragic experiences. I get to know their sadness and understand their hopelessness. Not surprisingly, depression is in a high percentage of my patients' diagnoses. After working with thousands of patients and clients, I began to see the root of everyone's problems. I could see the disconnect in their eyes and the lies that their egos have cleverly written for them. Many are walking around in shells that have so many brick walls up I'm amazed they can even move. Much like the children's movie in which society is moved up into space, with people sitting in motorized chairs propped in front of a TV, we are living in a world of disconnect.

We are all special. We *all* have a gift. The biggest problem is that we are disconnected from its source. Think of a dark room. You are standing near a wall and there is a big light switch to your right, and nothing else. All you need to do is reach over and turn on the light. When you do, you see so much beauty right in front of you. It feels breathtaking. But instead of doing this, many of us sit down, ball ourselves up in fear of the darkness, and close our eyes until the boogeyman goes away.

Our greatness is so close by and so powerful that it surprises me how difficult it is to connect to it. Yet it is. For me, my world of denial was so profound it was like wearing a blindfold and having someone else direct my life. I knew something wasn't right, but I had no clue what "right" was in the first place. In fact, I remember telling people that I just didn't feel comfortable in my own skin. I felt like I had hit a glass ceiling and had no place to go but down.

Then my divorce came. It was like a sledgehammer had jumped out of my back pocket and it applied the first blow to that imaginary barrier that seemed so unbreakable. Not that I was the one who had the courage to leave. Oh, no. My life of lies was so believable, I was sure I had the perfect marriage in spite of my unhappiness in it. My husband, thankfully (although at the time, I was not in the least bit thankful), had ended it first. He had set me free. He had allowed me to finally see who I was, and what my calling was supposed to be. He gave me the gift of despair and hopelessness so I could see my internal strength, which I now know as my light. He forced me to my knees to the point of such sadness and fear I had no choice but to surrender and be still for a while. In some ways, he was my cancer.

Did this awareness happen overnight? Um, no! In fact, it took me a good year of placing myself in other men's arms, drinking into the wee hours of the night, and scheduling my next good-looking victim. I had used sex as a cover-up to my reality. I just couldn't bear to see the real me. I needed to find some innocent guy to cover me up, tell me what to do, and let me slide easily back into my denial land that I knew so well. You see, my boyfriend Mr. Denial and I hadn't broken up yet. I still needed him. I wasn't ready to be set free.

I know many of you have been in the same place. I have met countless divorcees who did exactly as I did. I know the world is filled with addiction and we have all, at some point in our lives, become experts at hiding our true feelings. There comes a time, though, when what you have been doing just doesn't work anymore. You're fed up. You're done. You're throwing in the towel. You are shouting out in a darkened room in the middle of the night, *"I can't do this anymore!"*

So stop. And breathe. Just breathe. That's exactly what I finally did. A year after my separation, after countless men and nights of partying until four o'clock in the morning, I finally stopped. And I prayed. Who I prayed to, I wasn't sure at the time. I just knew I couldn't do this anymore. I just couldn't.

I knew that in order to finally begin my journey of finding me, I had to be real with myself. I had to let the cat out of the bag, so to speak. I knew I was good at hiding, so the first step was to stop the game of hide-and-seek and come clean. I wanted so badly to be happy. I wanted so badly to be real. Therefore, I had enough fight in me to take on the challenge to open up my shame box and let me see the damage I had done to my life.

So I began to *write* all my thoughts and feelings—anything and everything. I placed all of my vulnerability on the page and allowed myself to see my truth as it was right then and there. Was it hard? Heck, yeah! Was it worth it? Oh, yeah! You know why? Because I took away its power over me. I unplugged its energy source, which then allowed me to breath a bit better. And by doing so, I was able to then make room for something more worthwhile: the real me.

Exercise

The first step toward finding yourself is to start journaling where you are now. This is purely for you to see exactly who you are, in the present space and time.

- Write at the top of your first page: "Who I Am Now".
- Then begin to be real. Nobody will see this. Make this a safe journal that you know only you can see. This way, you can write freely, without worry.

The point of this exercise is to understand what is getting in your way. This is not about judgment, nor is it a time to beat yourself up.

This is purely a way to help you get real and stop ignoring the parts of you that you may be ashamed of. In fact, it is those parts that you are most afraid of that will help you get closer to your deepest truths.

- Write with as much honesty as possible.
- When you think you are done writing, commit to writing five more things. You may be surprised by what comes up.
- After you are done writing, put your hand on your heart, take a deep breath, and say out loud, "I love you."
- If that is too hard, begin by saying, "I will try to love you."

This exercise is the foundation for all the rest of the exercises in this book. Being able to honestly review who you are and love every part of yourself is so important, especially when you start to bring your skeletons out of the closet.

After you are done, go do something nice for yourself. Go for a walk in nature. Get some yummy chocolate or ice cream and reward yourself for a job well done. You are on the road to greatness, one step at a time.

CHAPTER 2

Self Love, Your Foundation

> *Today you are you, that is truer than true. There is no one alive who is youer than you.*
>
> Dr. Seuss

I remember the day I fell in love with myself. I was at the gym, sweating on the elliptical. I had my headphones on when a song came on about love. I have to admit that my pity party around being single was pretty loud at this point. I felt like a failure that I couldn't make my marriage work and even more of a loser that I was still single two years after my Big D. The negative tape in my head, or my ego "friend" (as it liked to remind me) kept pointing out that no one loved me and that I would remain single for the rest of my life. I found my days of depression were dependent on this conversation that felt like a scratched record stuck on the verse, "Nobody will ever love you...nobody will ever love you..."

When love songs came on, I would cringe, knowing that my internal bully was eagerly waiting to tease me about my sad life. But on that day, as I heard that song in my headphones, my inner spirit spoke up. I heard a voice that said, "Sing the song to yourself."

Now, that was a weird concept. Why would I sing to myself? I would much prefer to have a lovely man whip out his ukulele and stand outside my window with a sweet grin on his face, confessing his love for me. I spent my whole life looking for someone else to validate my worthiness and when he didn't show up or left on the next boat to *Movinon*, I felt crushed. Every time.

So when I heard that I needed to sing to *me*, this was a totally foreign concept. I could actually give *myself* the love that I had been craving for so long? The thought came that I was the most important person to love me. I lived with myself every day, didn't I? I had to look at myself in the mirror, put on my makeup, and cover my body in clothes. I already had to take care of me. Wasn't it time that I treated myself with the love a parent would give her child?

So I closed my eyes and imagined myself singing the song to my sweet little self. I sang to her, "I can't help but fall in love with you." I held her in my arms and kissed her on the cheek. I looked into her eyes and gave her the love that she so badly craved. We smiled with our hearts and drank in a love that was unconditional and pure. That moment felt like an eternity, but in reality it was an eternity in the waiting. I knew it was time to begin the process of loving myself. In truth, I felt sad that it had taken me thirty-eight years before I said those precious words, "I love you."

The reality is that many of us give love to ourselves last, if at all. We are taught to give unconditionally to others, but it is selfish to give to ourselves. We play words of self-hate and loathing on our negative tapes that, if shared out loud, would make us cringe in embarrassment for being so abusive. If there was such a thing as the Self-Abuse Police, we would all be in prison.

I saw an ad by the Dove brand that had women write down their inner dialogue. Then they had actresses speak those words in public so others could hear. It was truly eye opening for these women once they realized how mean they were to themselves. But we all do this. We do it until we learn to love ourselves and start speaking words that empower ourselves, not knock ourselves down.

We all know our self-hate words are hurtful, but we often say them with gusto. Many of us think it's the proper thing to do. If we feel bad about who we are, others will have pity on us. Others see it as a sort of competition of who hates themselves more. One of the funniest skits ever done by Monty Python was about who had the worst life. They each took pride and felt they needed to one-up the others just to prove how much their lives sucked.

And then there are others of us who simply feel we deserve our negative self talk. Whether it's from insecurity or a feeling of unworthiness, we take these mean-spirited words and let them seep into our beings. I even placed a megaphone directly into my ear. I would sit there feeling bloody and disheveled, preparing for the next punch. I felt like I somehow deserved these hurtful words.

There comes a point, however, when our bodies and our whole beings just can't take it any longer. As a nurse, I spoke with hundreds of patients about their lives. Most of my patients were facing life-threatening illnesses, such as cancer, or had dealt with chronic illnesses much of their lives. The common denominator with all of these people was that they had all hated some part of themselves. When I asked many of these patients whether they loved themselves, I got a resounding *no*.

That is why I am talking about self love so early in this book. It really is the first place we need to start. And that love must begin with your inner child. No kid deserves to be mistreated. Especially your sweet inner cutie who is desperate for your love.

I once went to see Matt Kahn, a spiritual teacher and author of *Whatever Arises, Love That*, who was teaching about our inner child. He said that no matter how much we try to become enlightened, our inner child will call the shots until we give him or her love and attention. Think of this child as the bratty kid who refuses to leave the store until you buy them something. Our inner child, for most of us, needs to be healed. That is why when I sang the song to my little self, I felt a love that was deeper than any love I have ever felt.

I have made it my mission to help others see how important it is to love themselves. It truly is the foundation to finding our shine. When we love ourselves, we are invested in our happiness. When we make ourselves our priority, we will do whatever it takes to heal. Often it's our self-loathing that keeps us from striving for a better life.

Loving oneself is a process. It does not often happen overnight. But when we do love ourselves, we begin to see life in a brighter, more positive light. Think about it this way: when we love who we are, we will forgive ourselves when things aren't going the way we want them to. We all make mistakes, and when we love ourselves we see those mistakes as lessons. On the other hand, when we are in a place of self-hatred or self-loathing we will beat ourselves down for days on end, never getting past what is only a simple mistake.

Another powerful technique for embracing self love is mirror work. I was blessed to have had the world renowned self-help queen Louise Hay teach me about the gifts of the mirror. Louise was famous for her work with affirmations and how saying them to oneself can have life-changing effects. She even carried a small mirror hidden in her bra. That way she could easily pull out her personal reflector and remind herself of her awesomeness.

I have personally taught this to many of my students and patients and I'm always surprised by how hard this work can be. Looking in the mirror gives us the opportunity to be real with ourselves. When I was learning from Louise, I was in a room full of other coaches and healers, and we practiced with our own hand-held mirrors. Yet when I looked around the room, I saw several people look around the mirror. It was as if looking directly at themselves was just too much to ask.

Our reflection is not something to be feared, but embraced. It may seem uncomfortable at first. Initially, I felt the need to critique my skin or my hair. Then I realized that this was what I did every time I looked in the mirror. I would find things wrong with me. I then made a conscious choice to change my conversation and to instead offer words of love and praise.

The most powerful mirror session came to me after a co-worker of mine told me she had breast cancer. I hadn't seen her in a while and noticed that she had lost a lot of weight. Being weight conscious myself, I wanted to get on her diet plan—until I learned it was due to the cancer.

That night I went home and had a nice chat with my body in the mirror. I knew it was time for me to thank my body and to tell it how much I appreciated all that it was doing for me. As I stood there naked in front of the mirror, I thanked all of my body. I even went as far as to tell the parts of me that I felt were the ugliest and told them that I was blessed to have these parts of mine still intact. I had my breasts, my arms, my legs, and my hair. I felt pretty lucky.

Most importantly, I had used words that were important to hear. I needed to say them out loud. I needed to look myself in the eye and give myself the gift of self love. I needed to finally say those three life-changing words, "I love you."

For many, these words are difficult to say, especially if you feel strongly that you don't love yourself. And that's okay. Start off small and say instead, "I will try to love you." Or say, "I'm thinking about loving you." Either way, this is a start and one that will begin the process of self love. Once you begin to love yourself more, everything around you will change.

We must always begin with ourselves. We must help ourselves before we help another. We are told to place the oxygen mask on ourselves first before we place it on someone else. Similarly, we need to increase our supply of self love before we start dishing it out to others. You will find that when you do that, you will have more love for others than you could ever imagine!

Once I fell in love with myself, my love for others exploded! I felt a love so strong for life and everyone around me. It was like I developed a super power once I put on that self-love cape. The best part was that the love came back to me through others. My love was being reflected in those around me (see my detailed discussion of this *mirror effect* in Chapter 7). Everything in my world began to change. It really did.

I hope you will see how important it is to love yourself and take these much-needed steps to building your own personal foundation of self love. You are worth it!

Exercise

Right now, go to your nearest mirror and begin to have a very sweet discussion about how awesome you are. If you can gather up the courage, say the big *I Love You*. I know this can be hard to do. If it is, say words that feel lighter, such as "I will try to love you."

- Make this your positive, loving daily routine, every morning as you are brushing your teeth or dressing.
- Each day it will get easier and you will find more things about yourself that you like.
- Consider putting up photos of yourself as a child on or around the mirror, to begin to heal your inner child as well as your present-day self.

I have put a guided meditation on my website to help you connect with your inner child. You can find a link to the website, where you'll find a page of all the guided meditations I offer, in the Resources section at the back of this book. Happy loving!

CHAPTER 3

No Judgment

Love is the absence of judgment.

Dalai Lama

Judgment is a funny thing. We all judge. In fact, we judge ourselves harder than anyone else on this planet. Yet I have learned a lot about myself since I started paying attention to all of this judgment stuff. For example, I went through a phase where I thought I didn't want a relationship. I was super happy in my life. I felt as if I were the envy of all of my coupled friends because I had freedom to do whatever I wanted and could sit around doing nothing without having to ask permission.

But the sneaky thing about judgment is that it shows you what you are hiding from yourself. Like a master of the game of hide-and-seek, I was hiding my true desires from myself because I was frustrated that they weren't coming to me. I packed my wants in concrete boxes and shipped them off to Timbuktu where they could never be opened.

Then I started paying attention to what I was judging in others. I would scoff at couples and immediately place judgment on them, convinced they weren't happy. How could they be happy with those fake smiles and "gross" public displays of affection? I would place bets on when they would break up and then hand them my card offering advice on how to be single. *Because I have to tell ya, I was an expert at that.*

One day, because I have always surrounded myself with brilliantly conscious friends, I was called out on my game. This judgment was helping me see that I *did* want a relationship. But because I wasn't in one, I made everyone who was coupled up "the enemy."

Have you ever done this? I would have to say you have. And please don't *judge* yourself for doing this. I have a heart of gold and care very much about people. Yet here I was, badmouthing a large percentage of the population, all because I was not willing to face my own truth.

So when my friends called me out, I was able to see with eyes wide open what I really wanted. However, without my harsh judgments on others, I might not have discovered these clues that finally got my head out of my ass, so to speak.

We don't judge to be mean—at least not to the other person. It is a built-in mechanism to help us see our truth. I saw a speaker once who spoke of just that. The funny thing is, I was judging her before she spoke. I met her the night before and remember thinking that I didn't think she was very friendly. I thought she seemed "stuck up and into herself." Then when she got on stage the next day, her speech hit me at my core because she was reminding me of a fear I had about becoming so big I would lose connection with others. And that's exactly what I was judging her to be—disconnected. Yet her speech taught me to recognize that our judgments are never about the other person. We have them to help us see our own truth.

Can you think of a time you judged someone? This happens a lot when we are worrying about our weight. I have a good friend who has a knockout body, but she admits she judges other people about the weight that they carry around their belly. She realizes this is because she is self-conscious about her own belly.

When I was in my twenties and insecure as all heck, I would focus on other women's hips. I was frustrated with my excess weight and was overly focused on my hips and thighs. So guess what I judged in others? Their hips and thighs.

The great thing about realizing the truth of judgments is that we are being blessed by them. We become more authentic once we realize that what we see in others is actually a reflection of ourselves. When we are preoccupied with our own shortcomings—when we are either "too little" or "too much" in some way—we automatically recognize that quality in others.

Step one to releasing judgment is to become aware of its source. Once we realize why we are doing it, we grow and open up to a truer, better version of ourselves. But we have to have the courage and self love to be able to do so. Beating ourselves up is counterproductive. And let me be totally frank with you: you are fallible, you will make mistakes, and sometimes you will feel like you suck. Guess what? We all do! We *all* feel that way sometimes. Just know that when you are beating yourself up, every person around you has been there/done that. They're probably doing it right now. That is why it's important to give yourself a break when you do something that does not appear in a very good light. Kiss that wound and move on.

There is a very strong link between how harshly you judge others and how hard you are on yourself. Self judgment is an even worse threat to our precious lives. That's why we also need to put a stop to negative self talk. The one area where I have continually beat my head on the ground with shame is my sex drive. I have not been proud of my sexual past. In fact, when I share my stories I fully expect others to judge me for my bad behavior and shake their heads in disgust. Yet that is not the reaction I get. It is only me who has beaten myself up. I have played the same story over and over again, only to realize that nobody cared. I was the only one who cared. Then I had to ask myself the question: What good is it to judge myself for doing something that is quite natural? My sex drive is a part of who I am, so why do I want to shame myself for being me?

That is when I decided I needed to stop this mental whipping and begin to see my sex drive as a part of me to embrace and not sweep under the rug in fear of not being seen in a good light. All of my partners were single like me. I didn't do anything wrong, but my judgment made me out to be a monster.

Is there something *you* have been hard on yourself for? It's time to allow that part of you that you've been ashamed of to finally come out. You are you for a reason. If it's something you feel strongly about (as long as you don't hurt anyone), stop hiding it. The only thing hurting you is you. I did that to myself over and over again until I got tired of suppressing my truest nature. And once I did, I saw the gifts of this passionate part of myself. No one has complained.

One final thought on judgments. The thing you judge most will keep coming up in your life until you let go of the judgment around it. This is the gift of the Universe to help you see the area that is in need of the most growth. Therefore, pay attention to the areas of your life that you keep coming back to in judgment. Then ask the Divine to take it from you and allow yourself unconditional forgiveness. When you let go of that judgment, then and only then will that repeated situation fall away.

Exercise

This exercise is designed to help you see more of your truth, not to make you feel bad for being a bully, either to yourself or to others. We *all* judge. But very few of us will take the time to learn how judgments can deeply affect our sense of well-being, and how removing them can be immensely life changing.

First take a look at how you judge others.

- Write down what you judge in others. Don't worry about anyone reading this. The purpose of this exercise is to get real and help unlock some of your subconscious beliefs.
- Leave some space under each judgment for more writing in the next step of the exercise.
- Some judgments of others might be: lazy, rude, superficial, boring, weak, shy, mean, fake, and so on. Don't hold yourself

back, but really consider actual judgments you know you tend to make about other people.

Now start looking at how your judgments of others might be a reflection of yourself.

- Under each judgment that you wrote above, write whatever comes to mind about what this judgment could mean about yourself. For example, if one of your judgments is that someone is too strict, has there been a time in your life when you didn't let your hair down and live a little? Did you ever want to do something fun but then decided that it would be too childish? If you can identify where in your life this might have come from, write it down!
- Take the time to sit with each judgment and write about how it relates to your own inner experience of life.
- After you have connected your judgments of others to qualities within yourself, write down your own glaring self judgments in a separate list. As in my own example, I harshly judged myself for my active sex drive and for not taking enough risks. How have you been most hard on yourself?

The final step is to look at all you've written. Look at each judgment, whether it is of yourself or of others, and start releasing it. Put your hand to your heart and say out loud: "I forgive you. I'm doing the best I can. I love you no matter what."

Releasing these judgments will dramatically change your life. What a great gift you just gave yourself!

After you are finished, go celebrate a job well done!

CHAPTER 4

Unconditional Acceptance

For after all, the best thing one can do when it is raining, is to let it rain.

Henry Wadsworth Longfellow

Now that you are digging deeper, I think it's important to note that "acceptance" is a word that is a must in your toolbox. Words have powerful energies around them, and even saying the words "I accept you" will give you some breathing room. On the other hand, non-acceptance keeps us stuck in the same rut. What we resist persists, and the only way to get out of the endless loop of shame is to learn unconditional acceptance.

In Matt Kahn's YouTube video, *The Way of Radical Acceptance*, Matt talks about how important it is to accept all of our feelings and emotions. He shares that not a single emotion should be shunned. We often tell ourselves that we "shouldn't feel that way," we "shouldn't think such mean things," or that we "should never think bad things about others or ourselves." Yet the energy of acceptance that comes with saying, "It's okay that I feel this way," will clear out any and all negativity.

Let me give you an example. Let's say you went out with a friend and they said something that made you mad. They had no clue they offended you. But it upset you and you went home and mulled it over in your head. You stewed over it for a few days, and then brushed it under the rug, and then you made nice with this friend. Then, months later, something triggered it and you find yourself even more upset, but now you don't even know why. This is because you never dealt with the original emotion that upset you in the first place. It has had time to grow and multiply in intensity.

This often happens in relationships. Couples get into fights and then bottle up the emotion. After a while, this small emotion is ginormous and you are now in couples counseling due to the intensity of these ignored feelings. I truly believe there would be less divorce if only we allowed each other to speak our truth and accept that we are all emotional beings who are fallible.

Our lives are filled with emotions that are brushed under the rug. In fact, many of us have so many rugs covering our feelings and filled with negative energy that we are really quite traumatized, often without even knowing it. I was never good about speaking my words toward my ex-husband. I would, instead, bottle those words and then feel like vomiting every time I saw him. Toward the end of our relationship, we weren't speaking at all. After we separated, it took me years to understand the trauma of our marriage. I was so good at hiding my emotions that it took some serious work to convince these memories to come out of hiding.

Words that we were unable to say during our childhoods are stuck in a water balloon that is waiting to be thrown. We fill our lives up with a masquerade of lies, just so we don't have to deal with our emotional past that we left in hiding. Many of us feel anger, sadness, fear, shame, and regret, but we don't always know why. Part of a therapist's job is to help us get those emotions out so they can finally be healed. Ignored emotions will always find a way to surface, often in the form of ill health or even life-threatening disease.

That is why it is so important to unconditionally accept *all* of your emotions. When you are feeling sad say, "It's okay." When you are feeling ashamed say, "It's okay." When you are feeling embarrassed say, "It's okay." When you are feeling judgmental say, "It's okay." When you are feeling angry at something say, "It's okay." In fact, my mom reminds me that anger, when not dealt with, turns into depression. That is why it's especially important to get that emotion out.

You see, we are human and as much as we don't like it sometimes, we are *all* of our emotions. There is not a single person in the world who doesn't feel this range of emotions. I don't know about you, but I've never met a baby or toddler who hasn't gotten pissed off at times. Even as young children we know intuitively that we must be who we are. Unapologetically.

Another form of unconditional acceptance is learning to accept others for who *they* are. I know this can be challenging and can sometimes feel impossible. As a parent, I always want to make my kids "better." I will do whatever it takes to protect them; but I've also learned that it's important that they find the tools to self soothe as well. I also do this with my partner, and I want to help him when he is down. The best gift I can give everyone in my life is acceptance. We all have a journey and it's important that we are allowed to be imperfect and learn at our own pace. My only job I have with the people I care about in my life is to accept who they are, and whatever state they're in, and to love them just the same.

Now, back to you. This gift of acceptance is something that will help to build the foundation of your life. Along with self love, with unconditional acceptance you will have the ability to withstand what comes at you with more stability. With practice, you will see how life changing acceptance is. Every day you will feel stronger and more resilient. Every situation will become a tool to help you become stronger. You will learn to honor your feelings and honor those around you, too.

I spent six months holed up in my house when I started doing this work. I cried a lot of tears. I yelled into the air and wrote mean letters to my ex-husband. I drew pictures that were dark and burned the paper in my fireplace with ritualistic vengeance.

One time I went for a walk, in the middle of my six-month isolation, and started to cry suddenly. I was walking through my neighborhood and didn't think much was on my mind. But since my focus had been to accept all of my emotions, I allowed the tears to flow. When I got home, I allowed all of it to come out. I cried like I had never cried before. The cries came out of my body and I shook uncontrollably. If someone saw me they might have thought I was having a seizure. I did this for about half an hour until there were no more tears to cry.

It was at that point I began to feel healed. I remember saying to myself, over and over again, "I will survive. I will thrive. I will survive. I will thrive." This became my new mantra and for the first time in my life, I knew I would be okay. No matter what.

You, too, can survive whatever comes at you. You have the strength to get through your past, and your tears will help you heal and let you live your life on your own terms. But first you *must* let all of your emotions flow through you with radical acceptance.

Exercise

In this exercise, you will practice accepting both yourself and others. Let's start with accepting yourself.

Look at all of the emotions you have shoved under the rug and tell yourself that you are okay. You will feel a huge weight being released from your shoulders. You may cry, or scream, or even want to run away and hide as you do this. It's okay that you feel *all* of those things.

- What words are you saying to yourself that are hurtful?
- When you recognize how bad they make you feel, say "It's okay" to yourself.
- Know that perfection is a falsehood, and that you *are* worthy of feeling okay.
- Keep looking deeply at how you've been talking to yourself, keep acknowledging all feelings that come up, and keep telling yourself, "It's okay," until you feel finished for now.

- Put your hand on your heart and say, "I accept *all* of my emotions; I allow myself to feel unconditional love for myself."

Now let's work on accepting others. It may take some time for your emotions to surface in this exercise. They tend to hide behind our logic and only come out when the logical voice is done talking. That's why it's important to keep writing, as directed below. The idea is to get past the point where logic will stop you from accessing your true feelings.

- Write a letter to someone you are mad at, or holding a grudge against. Don't write to share it with that person; use this as a tool to help you express your emotions.
- Write for at least five minutes and keep writing even when you think there is nothing more to write.
- When you are done, decide on a way to ritually dispose of this letter. You can crumple it; stomp on it; burn it; tear it into tiny shreds; whatever feels right for you.
- Put your hand on your heart and say, "I accept *all* of my emotions; I allow myself to feel whatever needs to come forward in this situation with unconditional love."

Enjoy the feelings of release and forgiveness washing over you!

CHAPTER 5

Your Body, Your Teacher

When your life falls apart you can either grow, or grow a tumor.
Lissa Rankin

As a nurse, I'm attuned to the human body. I have been trained to see what is "normal" and what is not. I see firsthand what the body can do when we don't listen to it. For the vast majority of my patients, when I ask them about their lives I can see why they ended up being so sick.

There are countless books detailing how our emotions can and often do affect our physical well-being. One of the best books on this is called *Mind over Medicine* by Lissa Rankin. As a doctor, she found that most people suffer ill health not strictly by chance, but rather by their poisoned minds. Through her research on placebos and *nocebos* (something that you think will negatively affect you, so it does), she presents a good argument that our minds play a role in our health. And when we stay in a state of dis-ease, our bodies will manifest with an assortment of problems.

On the flip side of that, your body can be used to help *heal your mind*. What exactly does that mean? The fact is, our bodies are set up to communicate subconsciously to our minds. There is a mastery within our cells that has direct communication to our higher self. Let me give you an example of what I mean.

A few years ago I was dealing with pain in my knees. It was in the back of both of them and got worse whenever I walked (and I *loved* walking). At first, I attributed it to switching exercise machines at the gym. But even when I stopped using the different machine, the pain persisted. It got so bad I would spend all my evenings icing and heating it, and I started popping Ibuprofen like it was candy. Being a nurse, I knew this wasn't good for my kidneys, but I didn't want to end up on narcotics in fear that I would become addicted like many of my patients. Nor did I want to seek medical advice. Lord knows I would never go through surgery, since I knew what complications that could lead to.

This pain lasted for about two years, and got progressively worse. I even consulted a physical therapist friend of mine who set me up with an assortment of exercises. But even they weren't working. Then one day I thought I would search for a deeper meaning in this situation.

One of the many things I have learned as a Certified Soul Coach® is that the Universe offers us signs in all that we do, feel, or see. If you run into a rattlesnake for instance, it could mean you are going through an important transition and increased energy is manifesting (I actually *did* run into a rattlesnake at my Soul Coaching training). Or maybe you find yourself driving when *every* traffic light is red and you ask yourself, "what does this mean?" Could it be that you need to slow down a little in life? (These are the exact words from my eight-year-old son when I asked that very question out loud.)

My point is that there are signs everywhere. And our bodies are no different in their ability to communicate to us and show us signs. I had a patient once who, at seventy-three years old, had throat cancer. He had had a successful career as a radiologist, was happily married, and had several children and grandchildren of whom he was very proud. In general he led a happy life. But then one night he told me a story about his mom and how he was still harboring anger toward her for something she said to him when he was fifteen years old.

His mom was long deceased, but these feelings of anger were

showing up as if this incident had happened yesterday. He had never had a chance to tell her how much she had hurt his feelings. It made perfect sense that he had throat cancer. He never had a chance to speak his truth.

He could look at this situation in one of two ways. One way is the glass-half-empty approach. He didn't use his voice and got throat cancer as a result. He could take that situation as "poor me, look where this got me." Or, he could take the glass-half-full approach and start the healing process. He could begin to use his voice to rectify the situation. Even though she was gone, he still had the ability to write out his feelings and express what had so desperately needed to come out.

He was relieved when I shared a technique with him to get his feelings out, and he was happy to begin the conversation that should have taken place fifty-eight years ago. I saw a weight lift off of him that he probably carried most of his life. All because he was able to recognize that holding back his words had manifested throat cancer.

Now, back to my knees. After I tried everything and nothing was working, I took myself to my meditation bench. I imagined some stairs within my body and I walked down the stairs to my knees. I then pulled up a little chair within myself and had a chat with the pain. I asked the pain, "What are you trying to teach me?" You know what I heard?

"You need to take bigger steps." That was it. Clear as day. And I knew immediately what it meant. I was not stretching myself far enough. I needed to take more risks and reach outside of my comfort zone. So that is exactly what I did.

The next day, I received an email from a group I had signed up for, but never went to, called the *Law of Attraction for Happiness*. The facilitator was stepping down and wanted to see if anyone would like to take over. I had never taught a group in my life and I had never been to this group in the first place. I had finished my Soul Coaching training about five months previously, but I was by no means an expert yet.

But for some reason, I knew this was the bigger step that I was to take. So I immediately sent back a reply and said I would take over the facilitation of this group. It turned out to be a huge success and has opened more doors than I could have possibly imagined. I reached *way* out of my comfort zone and did in fact take bigger steps. Then guess what happened to my knees? They have not hurt since, and it's been over five years. They are completely healed!

So you see, my body knew what I should do before I did. My body had the clues to guide my life. My knees were only hurting to teach me something. And as for my patient? He learned to speak his words and then to forgive his mom in the process.

See what beautiful gifts our bodies are? I now listen carefully when my body is hurting. In fact, I used to joke with my friends that when my neck was hurting, it was telling me to not go out with a certain guy. Even though my ego may have been enticed by some pretty blue eyes, my body sometimes told me to abort, abort!

My body speaks pretty loudly. Like a cosmic bullhorn, my body will keep shouting at me until I listen. I can fight all I want, but eventually I give in and listen, because it sucks being in physical pain.

Expanding on the saying, "Sticks and stones will break my bones but words will never hurt me," I now acknowledge that my broken bones can actually heal me. Kind of crazy, huh?

Exercise

What is your body trying to teach you? Have a journal nearby as you do this exercise, so you can immediately write down what comes to you.

- Get comfortable and scan through your body; notice deeply what you are feeling.
- Tease out the ache or pain that is bothering you most.
- Get quiet and ask your pain the question, "What are you trying to teach me?"
- Trust what you "hear" and sit with it for a while.

- Don't try to overthink what comes to you. Sometimes you may think that you are merely using your imagination. But often the lesson that you get is so profound, it feels like it couldn't possibly be from *you*.

If you have a hard time getting an answer, I offer a free guided meditation on my website to help you better communicate with your body. You'll find a link in the Resources section at the back of this book.

CHAPTER 6

Vulnerability

We cultivate love when we allow our most vulnerable and most powerful selves to be deeply seen and known.

Brené Brown

O ne time I decided to do a Soul Coaching session on my mom. She was in a new relationship and knew that he wanted to marry her. She was in town to visit me and shared that she was unsure about this courtship, but couldn't figure out why. He was a great guy and had written her love emails every day and tried his hardest to woo her. I decided that what would be best for her is to ask her higher power for advice, so I helped guide her to her spirit guide (which is also called a soul journey).

What came up for her was that she was not comfortable being vulnerable. She had been through relationships in which not much was asked of her, as far as vulnerability, and this man was wanting her to share all of herself.

What was interesting about this session was that I, too, was afraid of being vulnerable. My mom was my first teacher, and I have always felt like a mini version of her. But vulnerability is what truly connects us to others. In her book *The Gifts of Imperfection*, Brené Brown talks about how vulnerability is the key to living a wholehearted life. We are comfortable with people who are real with us, but in order to be real, we need to be vulnerable.

As you grow more into the real you, it is important to be vulnerable. Loving yourself also makes this process easier, and the connections you feel mirror back to you this love. Life is a dance best done when you show up being completely and unapologetically you.

I learned this lesson when I met my soul mate, Paul. Paul and I met when he started coming to my Law of Attraction group. We started out as friends simply because he thought I was out of his league and he didn't ask me out, so I thought he wasn't interested. Since we were just friends, we both thought we'd be completely vulnerable and lay out our dirt. We thought we'd have nothing to lose.

The amazing thing was that it was our vulnerability that made us see each other for who we were, and then we fell in love at the deepest level. And we thought that by being real and honest, we would be repelling love. Boy, did that backfire.

Showing up as your truest self and being vulnerable is how divine love is felt. We may all individually think, "If I open up, I'm going to get hurt again." Or maybe we think that if we share ourselves, we will be judged for the things we already judge within ourselves. So many of us think it's attractive to be "perfect" and put together. After all, isn't all of Hollywood perfect? I don't know about you, but the headlines I often see is that their lives are falling apart, they are getting divorces, and another young star either dies or ends up in jail.

The imperfections of this world are what we are attracted to. That's because they make us feel less alone in our own imperfections. None of us is perfect. Anyone who says they are is not being honest with themselves. People relate to others who speak with honesty. Tony Robbins, the famed self-help guru, attracts thousands of people to his events. In each one he expects people to get real and vulnerable, because he knows that is where the healing begins.

Vulnerability is truly a gift. But it's a gift that many shy away from. I especially see this with men. I had the good fortune to attract a lot of men to my groups and had allowed men a space where they could be open and honest and share their feelings. Having two boys myself, I know how important it is to raise my boys to be honest with their feelings and be allowed to be vulnerable and not feel like they need to "be a man."

I went to a workshop where author and speaker Tama Kieves asked the group, "Who grew up with parents who supported your emotions and let you be real with yourself?" I was one of two people out of fifty who raised my hand. I then tried this same question at my Happiness Coaching course with Robert Holden and asked the same question. Out of a room of about five hundred people, only about ten people raised their hands.

It's pretty obvious that we are taught from a very young age that it's not okay to show our emotions. We are taught to put on a mask and smile, even when we are falling apart inside. Then we are patted on the back for "keeping our cool," which then further reinforces that it's not safe to be vulnerable. Many of us have been hurt in relationships, so we train our heart to build walls. But it is these walls that keep us from feeling true love.

The one thing I love about being a nurse is that the majority of my patients who are fighting for their lives eventually find a way to take these walls down. In the wee hours of the night, I often have life-changing conversations with my patients. They all realize they have nothing to lose by sharing with me, their nurse. But the gift of this sharing is often that they get better.

I had a patient once who had neurological problems for which the doctors could not find a cause. They thought it might be meningitis, but they ruled that out. They thought she had a tumor, but none was found. After several tests and multiple hospitalizations, she was at wits end and was afraid for her life.

Then she was assigned to me, the nurse who believes in the power of our minds and our ability to self-heal. She shared with me stories of trauma that she hadn't shared with anyone else. She cried tears that had been sitting dormant for half her life. I allowed her to be vulnerable and loved her just the same. By the end of my shift, she felt better than she had in months. She was discharged that day and was completely healed.

Vulnerability is the window to the Divine. It is necessary if one wants unconditional love. It is something we are born with, but as we get older, many learn to think that vulnerability is an unfavorable trait. So we close our hearts, build walls, and wonder why we are unhappy, unhealthy, and chronically depressed. It often isn't until we are near our death bed that vulnerability forces its way back into our lives.

But don't wait until your health is bad. Chose to open your heart now and let others see you for who you really are. When you love yourself, no one can hurt you. So what do you have to lose? There is so much to gain. I found a love in a partner that I never believed could be possible, and it's because we both chose to be completely vulnerable.

Exercise

The eyes are the seat of the soul. Looking into someone's eyes is often uncomfortable. Why? Because by doing so we are being vulnerable and allowing them to see into our soul. I guarantee you will feel uncomfortable. But that is the point; vulnerability can be uncomfortable. Do it anyway!

- Find a friend or family member and sit across from each other.
- Hold hands and look into each other's eyes for one minute. Set a timer and stay with it for the full minute.
- When you and your partner are looking into each other's eyes, imagine love pouring out of you and into them.
- Then imagine the reverse. Allow their love to pour into you.

Once you get more comfortable with doing this, you will start to see the world with different, more compassionate eyes. You will feel the love that others are trying to give to you, simply because you opened up and became vulnerable.

CHAPTER 7

The Mirror Effect

The world is a mirror, forever reflecting what you are doing within yourself.

Neville Goddard

One of the quickest ways to get to know yourself and where you are in your life is by looking at the people around you. There is this mind-blowing thing called the mirror effect. The reason I call it mind blowing is because we are not taught to look at the world as a reflection of ourselves. We are instead taught that we are separate from each other. We are encouraged to go it alone and live in a mentality of "to each his own."

This separatist point of view is such a sad and limited way of thinking. I can't help but feel that so much of today's depression is because we are living separate lives yet intuitively know that we are all connected. And it's the disconnect that brings on depression.

Wherever you are in your thinking on this issue, remember that we are all made up of energy. When you see life as energy, and that everything you do affects others, you begin to understand how powerful this connection is.

A pool of water can serve as a good example. When a raindrop hits it, waves radiate outward from that point. Like that pool of water, when we are feeling something, that energy is then radiated out of us.

Whether we express it directly or not, others around us react to that energy.

The well known Japanese researcher Masaru Emoto came up with an experiment on how emotions affect water. He believed that when he spoke negatively or gave out negative energy to a jar of water, the water crystals would freeze into unpleasant shapes. When he spoke or gave positive emotions to other jars, their crystals froze into beautiful shapes.

From this experiment, we can see that our own energy is being felt and is affecting everyone around us. The benefit to this is that *everyone* around us reflects where we are on a vibrational scale. In order to receive all that we are asking of life, we need to be a vibrational match to what is in the *vibrational escrow*—the place that stores all of our desires before they manifest in physical form (more about this in Chapter 10). Most often, though, on a conscious plane we are unaware of how we are vibrating.

So the best and easiest way to know how you are vibrating is to look around you and ask yourself how other people are treating you. This is the mirror effect at its best. One day I was complaining to my friend Whitney that I felt people who lived on the east side of the river were unfriendly. I felt that no one smiled and didn't bother to take the time to get to know me. She, on the other hand, did not get that vibe at all. So she pointed out to me that they were just reflecting how I was feeling.

You know what? She was right. I was feeling disconnected from myself and being critical of where I was at the time. I was dealing with a lot of insecurity that manifested in front of me. This lesson gave me the opportunity to see what in my life was driving this insecurity. It also gave me the opportunity to see where I, too, had been unfriendly and was not reaching out to others.

I now look at all people as a beautiful tool to help me get real with what I'm feeling. If I'm judging someone, I now ask myself what I am judging in myself. If I get snappy responses from people when I ask them questions, I ask myself what in me is feeling impatient or grumpy. On the other hand, if the world is smiling around me and people are going out of their way to say "Hi," I know that my vibration is high and in receptive mode.

Think of your day today and how people around you acted. Were they easy going? Were they grumpy? Was there a theme? While it's true that we have no direct control over other people's behavior, it's surprising how our moods do affect what is around us.

Another important aspect of mirroring is how those around you reflect some of your limiting beliefs about yourself. Have you ever noticed that no matter what relationship you're in, you keep dating the same type of person? Or maybe that you keep getting the same kind of powerful boss who makes your life miserable?

These people are some of the greatest teachers in our lives. I joke all the time that my ex-husband is my muse. I have learned more from him than from any person in my life. He truly has been my blessing—not for what he gives to me, but for what he helps me realize I have taken away from myself.

In Buddhist teachings, it is said that your enemies are your greatest spiritual teachers. I couldn't agree more. They are the ones who reflect back to you your deepest fears. They help you see what your weaknesses are, and they provide you with an opportunity to work on your own reflections.

Our truest selves come forth through all difficult situations. We learn about our strengths and limitations. We find an internal power that comes out when triggered by difficult people. These people are providing you with a mirror, a tool to get in touch with what has been there the whole time. You just need someone to turn on the ignition so you can start moving forward.

The greatest parts of me came out through the tragedies of my divorce. I learned so much about what I had done wrong. I used this life-changing event to see that I was in fact strong, powerful, and resilient. I had the courage to see why this person came into my life so I could change who I had become, thereby getting more real with myself.

The world reflects yourself back to you to help you grow and become the best you that you were born to be. There are no accidents with who comes into your life. And when you begin to understand this, you can get out of the victim mode and into the growth and enlightenment mode.

I had a coaching client recently who told me about her frustrations with her boss. She felt he was domineering and controlling. He made her feel small, and she left work every day feeling like she had done something wrong. When I asked her if she has had other bosses like this, she said yes. Her last boss was the same. In fact, so was her ex-husband. Do you see the pattern here?

If you find yourself in a similar frustrating negative pattern, you could get mad and yell out loud, "Why does this keep happening to me?!" Or you can break the pattern once and for all when you see that these people have been reflecting some belief in yourself that needs to be dealt with and healed.

In my experience, I kept dating selfish men. I could have continued to default to the old "men suck" or "why me?" complaints. But that would have just kept those men coming into my life. Instead I began to see that these guys were just reflecting my old and limiting belief of "I'm not good enough, so please don't give me anything." You see, they were just showing up to help me reflect this false truth that I had been living with most of my life.

People are perfect reflections of how you feel about yourself. Navigating the single scene has helped me understand this truth. I can't tell you how many times I have sat across from a guy who was not a good fit for me at all. Yet there I sat, feeling hopeless and defeated. Then I realized what these guys were teaching me.

I started to ask myself what I needed to learn. It's no accident that I attracted this same type of selfish guy. Even though my self esteem was the best it had ever been, I was still stuck in this rut of mismatched men.

Then I came up with a theory. I came up with an awesome scale of 0 to 10, with 10 being a totally awesome person, and 0 being the ultimate loser. I asked myself where I ranked on this scale. My "now Michele" felt like about an 8, 9, or 10, depending on the day. I loved who I had become and thought I was a pretty great catch.

The guys I was dating were 4, 5, or 6. They were often a lot younger than me, jobless, passionless, and at one point I dated a guy who was a step up from being homeless. In fact, he was living in a city that had access to legalized medicinal marijuana to help treat his severe depression. I might add that I met him while I was in training to be a Happiness Coach. You see the irony? I sure wasn't picking the right guys, right?

So I began to ask myself: If my self esteem is so good and I feel pretty awesome on this scale, why am I picking the 5's or 6's? I realized that it was my inner child that was doing the picking. My inner child was sitting around a 4 or 5 or maybe even lower. That is who needed to be healed. And I am so thankful these guys had forced me to look within to see what needed my unconditional love and attention.

I began the process of healing my inner child and she caught up with my adult me in our awesomeness. I started picking 9's and 10's, baby! In fact, I was shocked with how quickly this change in quality happened. I no longer attracted a single low-scaled guy. I had raised my self esteem vibration, and now that pattern has been changed forever.

As you can see, this reflective world is absolutely mind blowing in how it can help you grow and teach you about your truest self. When you realize this truth, you will be thankful for *every* person who comes your way. You will no longer be a victim. You will no longer be stuck in repeating patterns, because you will see every opportunity as one to help you be a better you.

One last point I want to share about the mirror effect is this: you being *you* offers the world a perfect reflection for others. When I fell in love with me and connected to my truth, I could then offer a way for others to reflect *their* beauty into the world.

I often do an exercise with my groups in which we pair up, hold hands, and say to each other, "I'm here to be seen... I see you." I learned this in my Happiness Coaching training and it feels so good to look someone in the eyes—really look at them—and to have them really look at me. I have been told by many that when I look at them they feel like I see their deepest truth. Some have even been brought to tears by how I look at them. Once I had someone email me saying that even though they don't know me, they felt when I looked at them that I knew them completely. They didn't understand how I did that.

I now realize this happens because I am living my truth and am connected to my soul's purpose and self love. I am a perfect reflection of God. I have no agendas. I have no judgments or expectations. I only come from a place of pure love. Because that is how I feel about myself. My God self is open to the God in you. It is a beautiful place to be. And you are also capable of reaching this place. We all are.

My hopes are that you begin to see this world as a place to help you grow and shine the way you were meant to. Every day and every moment there are opportunities to help you see your truth. Each person is a blessing, and your love for yourself is a gift to the world.

Once you know this in the deepest part of your heart, you can be that perfect reflection for others. As the brilliant poet Rumi once said, "The beauty you see in me is a reflection of you." Be that perfect mirror. When you are, the world will only reflect back your beauty. I promise you that.

Exercise

This exercise is designed to access your memories of childhood traumas that may be unhealed, and this is a perfect opportunity to heal them. Current life situations can occur as repeating patterns, and once we identify these patterns, we can often eliminate them from our lives. I'm always amazed at how quickly negative behaviors can change when we recognize and heal the trauma behind them.

In this exercise, write whatever comes to mind, and remember that no one else will be reading this. It's important to get *real* and put all of the players on the table.

- Write a list of all of the people in your life who may have presented themselves in a negative way to you.
- Next to each name, write all of the qualities that these people have presented to you. Were they selfish, cheap, rude, stubborn, greedy, or some other quality?
- Keep writing to get it *all* out, whatever adjectives you need to use for as many people as you need to identify.
- When you are finished, go through your list and look for a pattern. Which qualities or behaviors come up frequently? Which ones strike a chord in you (that is, you feel a gut reaction when you see them written down)?
- After you have narrowed down your list to those qualities and behaviors that are recurring patterns, ask yourself this one important question: "What in me needs to be healed in relation to this behavior?"
- With each answer that you get, put your hand to your heart and say out loud, "I'm sorry. Please forgive me. Thank you. I love you."

This little mantra is known as *Ho'oponopono*, the very powerful Hawaiian Forgiveness Prayer. It will help you heal what needs to be released once and for all.

SECTION TWO

Prepare to Shift

CHAPTER 8

A New Beginning

Change is hard at first, messy in the middle, and gorgeous at the end.

Robin Sharma

One of the most interesting things about growth is that it is often a bumpy road. I have had several friends and students of mine come up to me recently telling me that they are finding themselves feeling really down. One of my friends whom I consider to be a guru in his own right confessed that he has even been having feelings of wanting to commit suicide. He would never do it, but the feelings are strong nonetheless.

And I get it. I really do. After I did my Soul Coaching training, which was completely life changing, I found myself massively depressed. This made no sense to me! I had released many blocks and had conquered many fears. I even dumped my boyfriend, Mr. Denial. I was on the road to recovery!

Yet I couldn't shake the feelings of insecurity, discomfort, and unsettledness. Then I heard a speech by Michael Bernard Beckwith, the founder of the Agape International Spiritual Center. What he said helped me understand why I was feeling so in the dumps. He shared that when we dig out what's old in our lives, we are left with a gaping hole. For a period of time, that hole is empty and feels uncomfortable. Why? Because it's empty. All that you knew before, all of your old habits, defense mechanisms, and poor coping habits are gone. Then you are left with a hole. But a beautiful hole at that!

Eventually that hole will be filled with your new life. Your new you. The you that has been dying to come out to play. Now that all of that useless chatter isn't taking up that space, you can fill it with all of your greatness. But that takes time.

Cynthia Occelli, author and businesswoman, has said, "For a seed to achieve its greatest expression, it must come completely undone. The shell cracks, its insides come out and everything changes. To someone who doesn't understand growth, it would look like complete destruction."

Growth is not an easy process. You can't expect to tear your world apart and walk away unscathed. There are bruises to heal, scars to mend, bones that need to rejuvenate. But the greatest part of all of this is the strength you will achieve by doing so. My ten-year-old son once told me, when he shared his frustration about living in two homes, "It's okay, mom. I'm going to become stronger because of this."

And you will, too. In fact, it is this in-between time that solidifies your resilience. There is an old saying, "God never gives us more than we can handle. I just wish He didn't think so highly of me." I would sometimes joke that God was using me as a guinea pig since He knew I would be teaching about survival.

Perhaps you are also being pushed so you can help others to heal. It takes one who knows suffering in order to help those who suffer. Personally, I wouldn't want to be guided by someone who hasn't been there/done that. I want to know that the person I'm going to for advice gets me. In fact, my favorite books are by teachers who have gone through their own trauma.

Right after my divorce, I read *Eat, Pray, Love* by Elizabeth Gilbert. I felt as though I had found a friend. I found someone who had been as low as me, cried as much as me, and showed me that she got through it.

That is why I'm writing this book. And perhaps someday you'll write your own book and heal your own people. But just know that when you feel low, sad, and hopeless, these feelings will pass. Something that I say repeatedly is, "This too shall pass." It never gets old and boy, does it help. There is no such thing as permanence. This too shall pass. That I know *for sure*.

There is another reason for the discomfort you feel after a massive overhaul has happened and you become more awakened to who you are. It's that you have stretched your emotions to a new level. Let me explain.

After I became awakened, which you can read about in Chapter 13, I found myself feeling such blissfulness that I could hardly believe it. I reached a level of joy I had *never* experienced before. It was not uncommon for me to start crying at the pure beauty of the world around me. Let's just say that my emotions were on happy overload (if there is such a thing). I felt a love rush through me and I felt unstoppable. It was almost like a drug. I wanted to be in this perfect place more than *anything*.

Then there came a day when I wasn't feeling it. I knew it was there, but I couldn't reach it. It felt like I was *giving up* on the blissful feeling that had been inside of me. I would go to my meditation bench and beg spirit to take me back there. But when nothing happened I found myself going into a deep depression.

Like my friend who I mentioned earlier, I had feelings of hopelessness to the point that I thought about ending my life. My emotions were erratic. I even went so far as to ask my mom, who is a licensed counselor, if I was bipolar. I went from one extreme to the other. Extremely happy to extremely sad; back and forth; up and down.

But eventually I started to stabilize. My highs started to be not as high, and my lows not as low. I found that I was okay with that. I eventually saw the whole process as necessary for my growth to fit into the real me. I needed to feel *all* of my feelings, the yin and yang, in order to appreciate all of me.

I was ready to live my truth and be accepting of every one of my feelings. In my Happiness Coaching training, I learned that the point of happiness is not to be happy all of the time, but to be okay with whatever emotion you're feeling.

Say there is a scale of 0 to 10, with 10 being blissfully happy and 0 being depressed and suicidal (as you've seen, I have lived all up and down this scale). The goal of life is not to be at 10 all the time. The goal is to be okay with whatever number you are on. It's really more about acceptance than it is about living a perfect life. Truly happy people know that happiness is not just about doing things they like. Happy people are curious, always eager to grow, and willing to move out of their comfort zones every now and then.

When we begin a "new life," getting uncomfortable is exactly what we are doing. And often for many of us, seeing our real selves feels really uncomfortable. For me, it has been quite a ride. And just as my brilliant son shared that his struggles would make him stronger, I thank God that I have become stronger because of mine.

You will, too.

Exercise

This exercise will help you learn to appreciate all of your life—even the down days, because that is where the growth occurs. This is an opportunity to practice nonjudgment and accept that your emotions are just emotions, not your enemy out to kill you.

- On that scale of 0 to 10, ask yourself where you are on the scale right now.
- With whatever emotions that come up as you evaluate how you feel, see if you can just *be* with them, without asking *why* you feel this way, or imagining that your feelings will kill you.
- If you are low on the scale, relax deeply and say to yourself, "This is where I need to be right now."
- If you are an 8 or 9, enjoy the feeling. Relax into acceptance of it, just as you would if you were lower on the scale.

- Feel the sense of being okay with *all* of your emotions—high, low, or in between.

Try to use this tool every day. Rate your emotions, and then sit with them. When you are feeling very low, imagine a dear friend sitting with you and holding your hand. They wouldn't demand that you snap out of it. And when you are near the top of the scale you can appreciate that time, too. It can be a lovely ride, knowing that you are growing while you navigate your emotional life in this way.

CHAPTER 9

Divine Guidance

> *Sometimes, when a tiny series of the most unpredictable events occur that make no sense at all, something big is about to happen.*
>
> The Universe (Mike Dooley)

The Universe is a powerful entity. Please don't take its power for granted. I know we all see the obvious strengths it exudes, such as earthquakes and volcanoes. But the power I'm talking about is what is in the space that we can't see. This ether, or universal energy, can be thought of as an energetic life force that is completely responsive to all of our thoughts and emotions. Beyond that, or really within that, is a multitude of helpers who are there to help you any way they can.

The book *Hiring the Heavens*, by Jean Slatter, was a life changer for me. She offers example after example of how the angels are available to help us. All we need to do is ask. I have used her strategy often and have often gotten what I asked for.

One time I couldn't find my son's Nintendo 3DS game (actually, my seven-year-old son couldn't find it and so it became my problem). Many of you know about these games; they are about the size of a silver dollar. It's not like you can trip over them, kick them, or have to move them off the bed so you can get in the sheets. No, this little bugger was hiding very cleverly, and my son's constant pouts about *me* needing to find it were driving me crazy. This search lasted for hours and I was almost ready to go to the store to buy another game just to keep my son quiet.

As I sat in exasperation, I decided to ask the angels to go find it for me. I had just finished Jean's book and I figured if it worked for her, maybe it would work for me, too. After I said out loud to my divine helpers to show me where it was, I got the intuitive hit to head toward my son's closet. I opened the door and saw a backpack hanging on the hook. I then instinctively reached in and voila! I found it! It was that quick.

It works for other people, too. My mom couldn't find an important document that was linked to some money she was entitled to after her husband's death. She had recently found out that she was going to lose this money (about $1,500) if she didn't find this important document. My mom was prone to losing things. And finding them easily was *not* in her nature.

So I suggested she ask the angels for help. I told her I would send my angels over to help as well (more help never hurts). That conversation was in the morning. By that afternoon, she had found the document. As a matter of fact, it was in the first box she looked in, after our conversation.

I use my angels for anything from helping me find things to getting me to work on time. They have come through for me more times than I can count. I now have an absolute belief that we are, in fact, helped and most importantly, guided. All we need to do is listen and pay attention to the signs that are being presented to us.

Life is a stream of "invisible" guidance. And when we become more aware of the signs and what they mean, the more fulfilled our lives will become. The truth is the angels, representing all of the Divine, want us to be happy. They want to see us succeed. They want us to live abundantly prosperous lives and will offer any help that they can. The problem is, most of us aren't listening. Actually, we don't recognize and act on guidance when we encounter it.

I have found that the Universe is always offering its guidance and support. But too many of us live in Ego-land, which is not directly receptive to divine energy. Why is that? To find the answer, it's important to understand vibration.

As spiritual beings, we naturally live at high-frequency vibrations. Those of us who are clairvoyant, or are psychically attuned, are better able to tap into the higher vibrational levels, which gives them an open door to what is beyond our human eyes. Most of us, however, operate at a much lower vibration, and the ego is often at the bottom of the vibrational scale.

The ego is that which tells us to be afraid, to be angry, or to feel ashamed. The ego questions everything and agrees to nothing. This ego is convincing and seems like your best friend. It will talk you out of a good thing in a heartbeat if that would threaten its existence. You see, the spiritual aspect of our being has no room for the ego. Therefore, the ego will do whatever it takes to keep you in its grasp and stay alive.

So when something out of the ordinary comes up that appears to be a divine clue, the ego sees the warning signs and tells you that you are crazy for believing it. But never fear, there is a simple solution to know which is right. In the battle of the ego vs spirit, when a situation comes up that you need guidance on, ask the question, "Does this choice make me feel light or heavy?"

When you've gotten your answer, go for the choice that makes you feel light. Spiritual guidance feels good. There is no guilt or shame; only feelings of excitement, joy, and most important, love. It makes you feel energized and unstoppable. When spirit speaks through you, to you, or for you, you feel more alive. The conflict arises when the ego starts to be threatened and starts trying to convince you to see things its way. It will fill you with doubts and fears, and those are heavy, negative emotions. But now you know that if a choice feels heavy, it's not to be trusted.

Once you become a better receiver of divine guidance and live more consistently at a higher vibration, you can start to see the clues that are scattered everywhere in your world. But the first step is to ask for help.

One day I was on a walk and was thanking God for my life. I was in awe of my success with my Law of Attraction group and my coaching practice, and I felt so blessed that I was making such a positive difference in people's lives. I was also thanking the Divine for helping me through my hardships and allowing me to show the world what true joy looks like (even when it felt like an impossibility at one point).

I had planned to talk about synchronicities in my group that night and just finished up some research in the book, *The 7 Secrets of Synchronicity: Your Guide to Finding Meaning in Coincidences Big and Small*, by Trish MacGregor. She suggests that you set the intention of seeing some synchronistic event and tell the Universe to produce it immediately. So, with the above thoughts in my mind, I set the intention that something would soon show up for me so I would know the Universe was listening.

I walked no more than half a block when my attention was drawn to a paper rose that was shoved in someone's retaining wall. I took it out and saw a note on it. To my surprise, the words written were, "Be the change you want to see in the world." I thought "Wow! That was fast!" But it didn't end there. I then went to an appointment with my son's doctor right after this and sat down in the lobby waiting to be called.

At one point, I looked up and was surprised yet again to see those same words framed on the wall. How fantastic is that? My ego could do nothing about that, by the way. I admit my spiritual self was doing the victory dance (she does that often because she is always right). This was also confirmation that I was on the right path. I took this story to my group so they could see how powerful the Universe is and know that guidance is real.

Once you start living your life wide awake, you will receive so much guidance you'll think to yourself, "How did I live without it for so long?" This guidance has come to me in different forms, and I invite you to start paying close attention to any and all things that come into your life. To help make it easier for you though, here are some categories where you could be looking for guidance.

Words

Whenever you set an intention or ask for universal guidance, be mindful of what is around you. The one place I have repeatedly found guidance is in words that surround me. I see it in license plates, advertisements, bumper stickers, and even the headlines of a newspaper being read by someone sitting next to me. In fact, the more I pay attention to what is around me, the more often I get an answer.

One time I was trying to decide about joining a mentorship program based in Salt Lake City. I asked the Divine to help me decide what to do and then set off in my car to pick up my boys from school. No more than five minutes later, I saw a license plate from Utah. Then, as if the Divine knew I was skeptical and doubted that this was a sign, I saw another Utah license plate moments later. Living in Oregon, that felt significant to me.

So I chose to go to Utah for the program and made some amazing contacts. I met people who have played a big role in my success and now know they are part of the divine plan to help me in my journey. One example is my dear friend Laurie who I met on that trip and who inspired me to finish this book. She is now one of my earth angels.

People

One thing I instill in my group members is how important it is for them to connect with each other. My group has grown by leaps and bounds, and I not only attribute it to the awesome guidance I have received, but to the people who show up who share their own brilliant knowledge. I joke that we will be taking over the world with how much fantastic energy is birthed in that room. It really is a powerful experience. Just as important, though, are the synchronistic bonds that are formed there.

I recently held a class where someone posted on our website that she wanted to come to my group but didn't have a way of getting there. Another member responded to say that she could ask other members for a ride. Then very soon after, someone said he would be happy to give her a ride since he lived nearby. It turns out he not only lived nearby, but they lived in the same building, same floor, and across the hall from each other. Talk about synchronicity!

I don't believe in chance meetings. I feel each person is sent directly from the Divine to help us on our path to greatness. Denise Linn, my Soul Coaching teacher, does workshops all over the world on past life regressions. She has often found that the strangers sitting next to each other have had similar visualizations and past lives. So it is no mistake that whoever comes into your life is there for a reason.

The Divine will bring you the exact person who has the knowledge that you are seeking. As it is often said, when the student is ready the teacher appears. This is really the Divine sending in its earth angels to assist in your unfolding.

Think about all the people in your life who have helped you. You will find more and more people coming to help you when you become more aware of your shine and are vibrating at a level that has no resistance.

I can't even count the number of earth angels who have come my way since I became clear on my life's purpose. When I was in Utah, I met a gentleman named Reggie Brooks who is a successful platform speaker. I know that my life's mission is to be a professional speaker, so I felt so blessed to befriend such a brilliant person. He has since taken me under his wing and is mentoring me. And we met when we both got "lost" trying to find the room where lunch was being served.

Pay attention to who you meet. Give yourself opportunities to meet people and set the intention that help is on the way. When you do, the angels move mountains, arrange plane tickets, and open up the roadways. All the work is done for you to meet that person. But you do have to be there to meet them. It's not likely they will come knocking on your door; especially if you don't open it.

Inanimate Objects

I love how I look at life now. I always ask myself, "What am I supposed to learn from this situation?" The divine is happy to help in your growth and will give you riddles that can open up your deepest limiting beliefs that are keeping you from being happy and/or succeeding. One such event happened to me recently while I was stuck behind a train.

I arrived in my car at the railroad gate just when the light changed and the gate came down. I thought to myself, "No worries. I have an hour and fifteen minutes before I have to be on that coaching call. I don't have to pee and it won't take that long." It turned out to be the slowest train I had ever waited for. I know that sounds like an exaggeration, but it truly was.

For fifteen minutes it chugged at a snail's pace and then abruptly stopped. Again I was counting my blessings. I didn't have to pee. I had time (although it was dwindling). And I had my Kindle so I had entertainment. I was a tad concerned about my phone dying, but at least my coaching call wasn't for another hour.

After about twenty minutes, the train started up again, and just when it was almost complete with the caboose in the middle of the intersection, it stopped again! I can't tell you how badly I wanted to push that train the ten feet needed to clear the roadway.

I continued to think, "I don't have to pee (I always count my blessings on that one), I have reading material, and I still have some time." The clock continued to tick, and tick, and tick. Another train went by in the other direction. At this point I wanted to yell, *"Are you kidding me?"* One woman even got out of her car and had someone take a picture of her trying to push the train (I'm obviously not the only one who thought this was possible).

I looked nervously at my phone and the time. My coaching call was about to start any minute and I was worried I wouldn't have enough charge on the phone to do the call. I managed to get on the call and tell my coach my dilemma, and he immediately asked me what I was resisting. I told him I thought it might be money, since that was a blockage I was working on at that time.

Right after I said that, the train finally started up again and all the drivers were free after a *long* hour-and-a-half wait! That train stuck on the track showed me that I needed to clear my money blockages in order to move any further. I learned that by living in my limiting beliefs, I will come to a standstill. The only way to move forward is to clear away these blockages.

The Universe is full of lessons and guidance. We just need to ask ourselves, whenever something irritating presents itself, "What does this mean? What is this trying to teach me?" I have learned more about myself in these kinds of situations than any other. The best part of looking at life this way is that you can take a seemingly bad situation and see the blessing in it. That is where the growth is, and will more than likely add to your happiness.

Numbers

I love numbers. It's like they are a secret code that leads directly to the Divine. Doreen Virtue, author and speaker, is world renowned as the "angel lady." She has written books, including the best-selling *Angel Numbers*, in which she discusses information she has received from the angels about the meaning of numbers. Even before reading her book or looking into the meaning of certain numbers, I had already felt, intuitively, that the numbers on the clock meant something to me.

For example, I always seem to notice 3:33 on the clock. I could be in the middle of something that has captured all of my attention and then, for some unknown reason, I will often look at the clock and it's exactly 3:33. And when I do that, I can't help but feel that it's the angels saying they are here for me.

Since noticing this pattern, I learned that, according to Doreen

Virtue, 3:33 means "the Ascended Masters are near you, desiring you to know that you have their help, love, and companionship." Talk about confirmation! At one point before reading Doreen's book, I sought out a medium who said I have a strong presence of the Ascended Masters in my life. In fact, she said she doesn't see that very often. I didn't even know what that meant at the time. But after learning about this powerful number, I couldn't help but feel that what the medium said was true.

The number 111 also shows up a lot for me. According to Virtue, if you see 111, or 11:11, you are to "keep your thoughts positive, because your thoughts are manifesting instantly into form. Focus only upon your desires and not upon your fears." I sure have manifested a lot in my life, and it was during those times when my desires were coming to me, I was in fact seeing the number 111 more often.

Start paying attention to the numbers that are shown to you. It's a fantastic way of staying in communication with the Divine without being psychically tapped into them on your own. I also believe that the more often you see these numbers, the more confirmation that you are on the right path.

All of the world is beautifully linked and the spiritual realm is always present to help thread everything together. Once you become clearer on your life's path, you will have more guidance than you know what to do with. Life will be easier and you will get a kick out of how the Divine is shooting messages to you.

You're on the right path, just by reading this book. Remember that when the student is ready the teacher appears. *Keep going*! You're on to something great!

Exercise

When we become aware of the guidance that is around us, we will often see more and more show up. So when you do this exercise, don't be surprised when you start finding more guidance given to you!

- Get yourself a little notebook that you can keep close at hand wherever you go.
- Take a day and set the intention in the morning that you will see some guidance from the Divine.
- Throughout the day, do all that you can to stay aware of what comes your way. Go for walks and look around. Trust your internal guidance and turn where you feel called. Go into places that feel right (remember "light" vs. "heavy.").
- When something happens that seems like divine guidance, write it down. Sometimes these events may not make sense right away. But when you write them down and compare them to the rest of your day, you may see a pattern.

I can see the Divine laughing now in glee that you are finally paying attention. Now it's time to see where it takes you. How fun that will be!

CHAPTER 10

Surrender

The harder you work, the harder it is to surrender.
Vince Lombardi

The greatest gift of connecting to your shine is that you start to listen to internal guidance more and trust that it has your back. The truth is, God has a plan for you far better than you can even conceive. Most of us are too bogged down with limiting beliefs to even let ourselves dream of the possibilities. That is why a big part of having all that you want is learning to let go and just let it in.

Abraham-Hicks is one of the best teachers on the Law of Attraction. I use their material in almost every one of my classes. For those of you who aren't familiar with Abraham, Esther Hicks channels Abraham, a spiritual being(s) (they often speak in the plural). She travels all over the world doing workshops where people can get on stage and ask Abraham any question at all.

The first time I heard Abraham-Hicks, they were on Hay House Radio, an online radio program with a delicious assortment of authors in the self-help, new-thought genre. I had no idea what Abraham was really about. I just knew I was very impressed, and I have since become a huge fan. If you want to know more about them, see my Resources section.

One of the best lessons that Abraham teaches is that all that we are wanting is already in "vibrational escrow (VE)." Every dream, every amount of riches, every ideal relationship is waiting for us patiently in this place that already exists energetically.

What exactly does this mean? It means that when you launch a desire, it then goes to this place of VE. Just like when you order an item from a menu in a restaurant and your order goes to the kitchen, your request goes somewhere until it's ready to be manifest. When you place your order at the restaurant, you then wait patiently for your food to arrive. It takes time to make your order.

While you wait, your only mission is to relax and have some good conversation, and then the meal will be brought to you. That's how life works as well. You launch a desire, it then waits for you to be a vibrational match (more on that in a minute), and then it *brings* to you what you've requested. But you need to be at a place to receive, which is often the hardest part for most of us. In fact, our trying to figure out the *how* of our lives will actually keep our desires away.

That's why I love the restaurant analogy. You place your order, enjoy your waiting, and then be ready for it when it comes. You wouldn't go barging into the kitchen right after your order was placed and demand your meal immediately, would you? When you want something that you are trying to manifest, you place your order, continue to live life in joy and in the flow, and then you get yourself positioned by way of inspired action (see Chapter 11). As with the chef, the Universe doesn't respond to impatient people. It's all about divine timing. And manifesting is as much about surrendering to divine timing as it is about inspired action.

I have taught several classes on letting go, since this is really the hardest part for most of us. And when you are trying to find out how to shine, your ego shouts at you to figure it out already! But this impatient stance is actually keeping it away from you.

The goal of any request to the divine, including having clarity on your life's path, is to ask for what you want and then do whatever it takes to let go of the outcome. It's not that you're letting go of your dreams. You just put your trust into something greater. You are taking away that expectation that says it has to look a specific way. Believe it or not, the Divine has a far better plan for you. That I can say for sure.

I had only gotten involved with the Law of Attraction because I was tired of being single. But what I got when I surrendered and trusted this ride was a passion that I had no idea existed in me. In fact, my ego could never have thought up this brilliant plan. Why did it come so quickly to me? It came because I trusted that something greater was waiting for me, but I didn't carve what that would be into stone. In fact, one of the most powerful phrases you can say to yourself is, "This or something better." This attitude can change your expectations into an ability to accept all the gifts—without resistance—that the Universe wants to bring to you.

I have surrendered, and continue to surrender, to the Divine's plan and trust that it is going to lead me to some amazing places. I have been to a couple of Hay House events, including an *I Can Do It* conference in Pasadena, California. I was inspired by the speakers who had shared how they got from point A (often a place of misery and pain) to point B (on stage, writing best-selling books, and inspiring people). The common denominator with all of them was being able to let go and see where life would lead them.

Most of the speakers shared stories that helped me see that the steps they took could have never been planned. In fact, most plans were eventually thrown out. The divine plan was the only one that worked.

Many of us say we have trust in the ether, which I wrote about in Chapter 9. We believe that we give control to God and say we aren't worried that we won't get what we want. But then I hear people say things like, "I mean, it's been a couple of weeks... where is it?" As Americans, especially, living in such a fast-paced world, we want everything now. So waiting for many of us is hard. I get that.

Yet built into this time of waiting is the journey of expansion that occurs with every trial and tribulation that comes our way. It is those moments of failure that add more clarity. It is those times of doubt that give birth to the opposite of what we do want. We just need to appreciate these times of "waiting" as the gift that they are. This is also the time when we can learn to let go and really give our trust to the higher parts of ourselves that will guide the way.

At the beginning of each year I do a vision board class with my group. What I love about vision boards is that they help us get clear about what we want, we place it in our constant conscious view, and then trust that it will be brought to us. Most, if not all of my mentors and coaches, and favorite authors—including Wayne Dyer, Louise Hay, and Jack Canfield—have done these life-changing boards.

There are countless success stories of people who have manifested what they put on their board. In fact, I did one for a house. I had decided to buy a house after renting for four years after my divorce, but had no savings, had credit card debt, and had told the entire world that I was never going to buy a house again.

So when this thought of, "I'm going to buy a house" came up, I felt ill prepared. But knowing the power of these boards, I got to work. One thing I have to say is how much fun they are. I usually put on some good music, grab some of my favorite magazines, and allow myself to dream. It makes me feel like anything is possible, so it's one of my most joyful activities.

After I finished the board, I released the outcome to the ether. As with every vision board I create, I wrote on it, "All that is here is so, and I thank the Divine for bringing me this or something better." I put the board up on my shrine, which at the time was above the fireplace in view of where I often sat. That way I could keep my conscious mind focused on what I wanted.

Did I obsess over it? No. But when I looked at it, I felt joy and excitement, and that is an important quality to cultivate when we want to manifest our desires.

The next day, I got an email from one of my group members asking if I had found a mortgage broker yet. I had emailed my group to say that I was thinking of looking for a house, so she reached out to me. I hadn't even gotten that far. I had only just decided to buy a house the day before, and my vision board was completed that same day.

So, the first part was sent to me—a mortgage broker. Then it was time to start the search. Because of my busy life and the fact that I felt no rush, I hadn't even gotten as far as finding a realtor. I did, however, begin looking online for houses, but I didn't even take that search too seriously.

One day I went to a forested park on the other side of the river from where I was living at the time, to go hiking with a friend and our kids. This is not an area we ever go to, so I was surprised by how beautiful it was. Then I thought to myself, "I wonder if there are any houses for sale here?" I got online and found the cutest house that was backed up to the forest. I have always loved nature, and the idea of being surrounded by it seemed like a dream come true.

My mortgage broker recommended a realtor to me, and I told the realtor that I wanted to see the house. The next day I saw the house and fell in love with it. The day after that, I put in an offer. Within two weeks of having planted the seed of wanting to buy a house, I had bought my dream home.

The most amazing part of this, besides it being so ridiculously easy, was that on my vision board were so many similarities to the house I bought, it was astounding. In fact, my boys' room was practically identical to the one on my board. I also put two sheds on my vision board, and as you might guess, my house came with a quaint shed in the back yard. This all happened so fast, I didn't even realize the similarities until someone pointed it out.

The power of the vision board is twofold. First, it gives you clarity about what you want. When you are trying to manifest your shine, you first need to ask yourself how you want to feel if you were living your soul's purpose. Find pictures and quotes that help you access this feeling and make this a powerful picture in your mind.

Second, it helps you let go. There is a power to these boards, and time and time again I have seen them work. If you understand this belief, then it is easier to trust that your desires will manifest. And when you trust and let go, you are better able to let in what's coming to you.

As I mentioned earlier, there is a thing called "vibrational match." Let me explain this now, because this is important to understand in order to manifest. When we want something that excites us, it goes into that energetic space of vibrational escrow. Our job then is to be in a place of receptivity. We need to keep our vibrations high so that what we want can then match up to us, thereby allowing the manifestation to come into the physical plane.

What most of us do, though, is worry about why our manifestations haven't come to fruition. How does worry look vibrationally? It's on the low end. In fact, any negative emotion—such as fear, sadness, guilt, shame, impatience, and hopelessness—will keep these dreams away from us. But feelings of joy, happiness, excitement, and hope are a better match to what we desire. Chapter 19 in this book is all about joy, because I believe having joy is so important in all that we do.

Surrendering to the Divine is very powerful. It helps us let go of those negative emotions so we'll have more room for the positive ones that will bring us what we want. Have you ever thrown your hands in the air and said to yourself "I give up!"? Didn't you feel a weight lift from you? The same can be done when we surrender our negative emotions to the Divine.

I know I wouldn't have the life I have now if I hadn't given the control to my divine guidance. The people, books, and situations that have flowed to me are the direct result of not getting in my own way. So I encourage you to get out of your own way, too, and see what greatness is awaiting you.

Your shine will get brighter and clearer when you trust that your greatness is part of the divine plan. The "manager in the sky," as Abraham likes to call it, wants nothing more than to help you. And wouldn't you want something that has the power to move mountains on your team? I have help every step of the way. You can have it, too, and all you need to do is ask for it and let it in.

Exercise

Creating a vision board is a powerful exercise that will change your life! The instructions below are for creating a physical board. As you go through this process, I encourage you to approach it with joy and excitement about the unlimited possibilities for your life!

- Gather some of your favorite magazines and start cutting out pictures and words that resonate with you. If you don't have any, ask friends to donate theirs. Or you might even find an inexpensive collection of magazines at Goodwill.
- Get a board that feels right to you. It can be big or small, depending on your preference. Personally, I like to use a mid-size board with a firmer backing so I can set it up on my mantle or in front of my meditation bench. There is no right or wrong kind of board to use, or way to use it; just do what feels right.
- Once you feel finished with gathering the pictures and words you've cut out, place them on the board in whatever way your soul guides you. There are no mistakes when arranging your images and words on the board. Your subconscious mind will direct you to place them where they will give you hints about your deepest desires. When you're happy with the arrangement, use a glue stick to permanently put them in place.
- After you are done with your board, write on the back, "All that is here is so, and I thank the Divine for bringing me this or something better." It's important to show gratitude in all that you ask for. First, gratitude helps you to feel good. Second, when you say thank you, you are expressing the belief that you have *already* received what you're asking for.
- After expressing your gratitude, place your board somewhere where you can see it often, so that it will stay frequently in

your conscious awareness. This will also serve to remind you of the joy you felt as you were creating it.

Have fun with this and don't limit your imagination!

Another option is to use the Hay House Vision Board app that is available for iPhones. In a couple of minutes you can create a fantastic vision board to use as wallpaper on your phone, and you can easily share it with friends and other Hay House app users.

CHAPTER 11

Inspired Action

> *You may never know what results come of your action,*
> *but if you do nothing, there will be no result.*
>
> Mahatma Gandhi

One of the biggest challenges for our human minds (ego) is the idea that we always need to figure out what we're going to do. We plan our days with such intensity, there is often no room for spontaneity. We plan our days off. We plan our careers. We plan our kids (well, maybe not always), our houses, and the white picket fence. I remember walking through a beautiful neighborhood, thinking about all the steps that I needed to take to buy one of these houses. I needed to get my degree. I needed to find a good job. I needed my husband to also find a good job. Then at the end of all of this—voila!—there would be my perfect life. Then life turned upside down and backfired. Not only did I not get my house, but at the end of the day, or decade, I didn't even want it!

Our egos like to get out the calendar and demand that we place something on it. There always needs to be a plan... or two... or three. That is why it's so hard for us to let go and let the Divine call the shots. In fact, the powerful "manager in the sky" has the most fabulous life planned for us. Our only job is to chill the f..k out. When we do, then we can listen to the signs and let the Divine inspire us to action.

Part of the fun in life is to follow the breadcrumbs and see where it will take you. The ego will protest because it needs to have detailed instructions on the workings of your day. My best advice is to pat it on the back and say, "Thanks old friend, but I got it." Or better yet, "God (the Divine, Source Energy) is driving. I'm just going along for the ride." Then offer a little dance move—because it's fun. At least that's what I do. Feel free to do anything that makes you happy in the moment. The ego is always tripped up and distracted by spontaneous fun.

You see, our forward movements are best guided by our higher power. It's our job to listen and then take inspired action. Passion is the *result* of action, not the cause of it. We must move so that we can see how life is meant to play out; but only when we are inspired by the Divine, because that is the yellow brick road to greatness.

Here's an example of inspired action. Say you wake up in the morning and slowly begin to start your day. Then you may turn on the radio, check out Facebook, Twitter, Instagram, or whatever social media that appeals to you. As you go through the newsfeeds, something pops out at you and gives your body a jolt. Suddenly, you have an idea. It may be small, or maybe it is the "ah-ha" that you have been searching for.

At this point you have two choices: do something about it, or do nothing about it. Inspired action will be driven by this "crazy" notion that you should take action, even when it doesn't completely make sense. Most people shove these moments of inspiration aside because they think they need more data, more research, or more "signs" that this is the right move.

But life gets more interesting when you just say *Yes* and then see what happens. All of the great moves in my life have been inspired by something greater than me. How do I know that I had a divine tour guide? Because the guidance I received was a little crazy; a little scary. And it made me jump out of my skin with excitement. Luckily, I've always listened and taken action on this guidance.

One such action was when I was beginning to write my first book (unpublished) and I hit a roadblock. I let my ego convince me that nobody would want to read what I was writing. I was not even a writer, so what the heck was I doing? I decided to go for a walk, fought back tears behind my sunglasses, and hoped that my sobs would not be heard except by the trees. Then I got a text from an acquaintance of mine, who was a writer, asking how I was. Normally I would just ignore this type of message, since I don't like to be seen in that state with someone I hardly know. But I felt the urge to be vulnerable and reply to him in honesty by saying I was doing terrible. Then he texted and asked if he could call. I surprised myself by saying yes, even though I was embarrassed that I was falling apart.

When he called, I shared my frustration about being hijacked by my ego, and he started laughing. He wasn't laughing to be mean, but to let me know that he has felt that way at times, himself. In fact, we all have! I really needed this pep talk and went home from my walk with a new heart.

When I got home, I went through my mail and saw a flyer for a writers workshop being held by Hay House that coming weekend in San Francisco. It just so happened that I had the time off and didn't have my boys, since they were at their dad's. So I went, and what a divine experience it was! It was there that I heard advice from angel expert and author Doreen Virtue. She also had started her career with two young boys, had followed her intuition, and did what she was called to do. She explained that we each have something in us that needs to be shared with the world. And no matter how hard we try to ignore this urge, it will keep tapping on our shoulders until we listen. But we must act on these notions. We must follow these inspired steps.

Think back to a time in your life when you were inspired and acted on it. Even as children, many of us have been inspired to take up a sport, or take a class that may have changed our life. When you look back and see the steps needed for the things that went right in your life, I bet you'll recognize that it was your intuitive spark that made it happen. I would even suggest that when you write down these amazingly awesome events in your life, you will see that these were divine pushes.

You may be asking now what the difference is between *inspired* action and just plain old action. Well, let's talk about love and fear. I'm sure you recognize that these are two very different feelings. When we do things out of love, we may feel excited and giddy, or deeply moved in a positive way. Our energy shoots to the moon. We feel invincible and fearless. Love is the most powerful force there is. Therefore, it's a good feeling to heed.

Fear, on the other hand, feels draining. It feels stressful and makes us feel anxious and powerless. When we are in fear, we are reactive and move simply to avoid something negative. Acting out of fear feels like walking through sludge; like trying to swim upstream and tiring out very quickly. So many of us just give up at this point.

Divine presence is pure love. When we wonder if we are receiving guidance from the Divine or not, it's important to ask: is it love or fear that I'm feeling? If it feels like love, listen to it. If it feels like fear, take a deep breath and hang tight. No action is needed (unless you are being chased by a grizzly bear!). Inspired action will feel like love, and knowing the difference will help you take action when it is necessary.

The best way to tap into this angelic stream of divine guidance is to do whatever you can to raise your vibration. Then, when you get excited about something, simply say *Yes*! Say *Yes* even when you don't have a plan. Say *Yes* even when those around you are telling you that you are crazy. Say *Yes*, because you never know what is behind that curtain until you pull back the drapes. If you follow the steps that I've outlined in this book, you will be better prepared to trust this divine inspiration. Then watch your life soar as it was always meant to.

Exercise

This simple exercise is designed to help you practice listening to divine guidance and taking inspired action.

- Commit to a day when you will try to see where the Divine takes you.
- Go to a bookstore and follow your intuition as to what books interest you. Say to the Divine, "I'm open to whatever you ask of me. I will listen to your guidance and I will say *Yes* when you ask me to act."
- Then walk around and pick up whatever book you are drawn to.
- The next step will reveal itself only after you have taken this first step.
- Say *Yes* when you feel moved to take each new step.

Don't question this process. Only trust that you are guided to the next move, and that is the *only* thing that should concern you. And remember, is it fear or love calling you? Love should be the only thing that moves you.

Steps to Transformation

CHAPTER 12

Declutter

*The only way to get what you really want is to let go of
what you don't want.*

Iyanla Vanzant

One thing I have learned about life is that our inner and outer worlds affect each other. In my own life, even with all of the inner growth I made, my outer world always seemed to be out to sabotage the great work I had done. When I was beginning to identify the real truth of myself, and made happiness my priority, I had to put a wall up to keep the boogeyman out. Sadly, in this real-life fairy tale, the boogeyman was not a man at all. He was not even human. He was all of the clutter that clogged my energetic space. "He" was the weighted-down crap that suffocated my being. Unfortunately, I didn't realize that the stuff in my house and my life was preventing me from growing until I began training to be a Certified Soul Coach®.

My Soul Coaching teacher, Denise Linn, has made decluttering one of her passions. She was the first person to write a book on feng shui in the United States. She is known for her Space Clearing work and was even asked by Oprah to be a regular consultant on her show. I feel blessed to have learned from the best, and I've found decluttering to be life changing.

Why would this be the case? To begin to answer that question for yourself, look around at your surroundings. No matter where you are, whether you're at work or at home, how do you feel in your environment? Do you feel relaxed? Comfortable? Peaceful? Tranquil? Or do you feel smothered? Weighted down? Uncomfortable? Stressed?

I recently got rid of a futon that I had been holding onto for years. I had never thought much about it until then. I felt a huge weight lifted from my shoulders. It was then that I realized that my ex-husband and I slept on that futon in the beginning years of our relationship. I hadn't even realized the negative effect it had on me until I got rid of it.

The items in our house affect our energy. Let's talk about energy for a minute. Scientists have recognized that we are all made up of energy. In the world of quantum physics, everything is interrelated, and everything vibrates at its own frequency. We have an emotional link with most items in our home, whether subconsciously or consciously. When we have a negative link to an item, the energy of that item vibrates back to us and zaps *our* energy. Conversely, a positive link to an item can light us up.

Each item in our home emits its own vibration, which can either zap our energy and make us feel down or ignite a glow that lifts us up. For example, say there is a picture on your wall of a family photo taken at a time in your life when you were unhappy. Every time you walk by that photo, whether you are aware of it or not, you are absorbing the sad emotions from that time. Or, on the other end of the spectrum, say there is a flower vase sitting empty in your glass cabinet, which was given to you by a dear, respected friend. Do you see what a difference these two items can have on your life?

When I moved out of my marriage, I literally decluttered my entire life. I insisted on buying everything new. I felt lighter than I had ever felt, and this decluttering process really helped me feel like I was starting fresh; starting anew.

Several years later, after my Soul Coaching training, I decluttered again and started weeping as I emptied the kitchen cabinet. Little did I know, until then, that those items that sat in the back reminded me of the trauma of moving out. They were among the first items that I had unpacked when I started my new life.

The point here is to notice how much your home and surroundings affect you. *Everything* around you has the capability to either lift your spirits or drag you down. When you begin the process of connecting with your true self, you can create that fresh canvas for yourself and begin your new work of art; one room, one drawer, one shelf at a time.

When you go through this process, I guarantee you will feel lighter and will notice an increase in your energy. Why else do they say, when you decrease your stress, that you "lightened a load off of your shoulders"? Decluttering the things in your life will change your energy and help you on the path toward true happiness and enlightenment.

It's also important to "declutter" toxic people from your life. Most of us have family members who are in our lives by default, but we would be much happier without them. I suggest that if they make you feel bad when you're around them, put up your "Do Not Disturb" sign. Find a way to distance yourself. Make yourself busy. Fill your life with so many good things that you won't have room for those who aren't good for you.

Is this mean? No. We are not responsible for others' happiness. The people you want around you are those who enjoy you for who you are and will do whatever it takes to help you on your positive life mission. Even if they offer just an open ear and a smile of encouragement, those are your team players. The one thing I really love about the Law of Attraction group that I teach is that we are a community of positivity and joy. It really is an exciting place to be. I am so blessed by having my tribe of inspiring friends.

The magical thing about life, I have learned, is that when you begin the process of self love and make a stand for what you deserve, the negative people fall away and the positive people show up in droves. This is the natural outcome of raising your vibration. But it's important when you are first connecting with your shine that you make a conscious effort to eliminate the negative and increase the positive. I call it my *No Negativity Zone*. During this phase, you can think of yourself as being in your cocoon before you break free into being a butterfly. You need to protect this newfound you until you are ready to let your wings be free. And when you begin to fly, your tribe will be shining as brightly as you are.

One last aspect of decluttering your life is to be watchful of what you are feeding into your mind. In the powerful book *The Slight Edge*, author Jeff Olson equates his success to his daily regimen of feeding his mind with positive, enlightening material. He begins his book by pointing out that if we took all of the negative books we read, or news stories we pay attention to, and instead feed ourselves more empowering messages, we would be successful no matter what. His underlying philosophy is that if we read something positive just ten minutes a day—every day—we will see our lives transform.

This book struck a chord in me. I read this book several years ago, and realized that this very simple act could have dramatic effects on people's lives. I found that it wasn't hard at all to read ten minutes a day. And case in point, my life has changed dramatically since then.

Connecting with our shine is a delicate mission. Our minds are our sacred temples that must be handled with care and love. Our inner world will grow if our outer world offers us the support we deserve. You wouldn't want to water your seeds with poison, would you? It's time to give yourself the nourishment you deserve.

So take out the trash, and I mean all of it. And flower your world with people, things, and media that help you to shine like diamonds. Happy decluttering!

Exercise

This exercise is designed to help you learn how the vibrations of the things that are in your life affect your emotions and your own energy levels.

- Pick the most prominent room in your house (the one you spend the most time in) and start walking around in it.
- As you pass each item, picture, or piece of furniture in the room, take a deep breath and pay attention to how your body feels.
- What does your body do around each item? Do you notice yourself wanting to look away? Or do you feel a more loving vibration around it?
- As you touch each item, ask yourself, "Do I feel light or heavy or neutral?"
- If you notice a heavy feeling in your body, and if it's a small enough item, put it in a box. Obviously, you can't put furniture in a box, but take note of how it makes you feel—you might want to decide later what to do with it.
- With the smaller items that make you feel "heavy," don't overthink or rationalize what to do about them. Just take action and put them aside. You don't have to commit to giving them away or selling them. But taking them out of your energy field will make a big difference.

When you are finished with this exercise, reward yourself with something positive. Positive reinforcement *always* helps to reward any efforts we make toward improving our lives. Whenever I have done a decluttering, I have gotten something special for my shrine for meditation. These items serve as reminders of my commitment to myself. You deserve such self love, too!

CHAPTER 13

Meditate

> *Meditation practice isn't about trying to throw ourselves away and become something better. It's about befriending who we are already.*
>
> Pema Chödrön

A big step in getting real with ourselves is to take a much-needed pause, sit in silence, and listen. I did this through meditation. I did a lot of research before I took action and put my lessons to the test. I went to Buddhist temples, took meditation classes, read books, and watched YouTube videos. I thought a lot about it and even set a room aside in my house dedicated to my meditation practice.

I envisioned myself being like a Buddhist monk, meditating for hours and levitating into the sky. I saw myself becoming an expert and one who could live a truly mindful life in which even the Dalai Lama would ask me for advice. I would be the enlightened one. I would be a meditation rock star. I only had to finally do it! Lesson one. In order to meditate, one must do it.

This went on for about six months—this mental workup without action. Why was I not sitting down, closing my eyes, and listening? In truth, I was terrified! I was afraid of what might come up. I was sure that my feelings were bigger than me. I was scared that if I saw my truth, I would die in shame. I would die a slow, tortuous death as my deepest fears would send out a poisonous gas that I would be forced to breathe in. Mr. Denial kept whispering in my ear, "Don't do it. Stay with me, honey. I will protect you."

It was at the point when I had the choice of living my life as it used to be, or living a new life that I was just beginning to dream about, that I finally sat down. And I breathed. I just breathed.

I began slowly at first. I experimented with all that I had learned. I found that my monkey mind, as many call it, was way too distracting. I envisioned a baseball bat hitting those thoughts that came streaming my way. I became a homerun hitter! I had lots of practice with that bat.

Then I tried to focus on a candle, a rose, the wall. I put on meditation music and tried to chant Om. I used mantras, counted my breath (the practice where you count until you get lost in thoughts then start over again. I rarely made it past three!). I tried open-eyed meditation; facing-the-wall meditation; cross-legged; lying in bed. Then I finally settled onto a meditation bench with a pillow below to support my feet.

As you can see, I was determined to make this work. At times I found the task of meditation too stressful to complete. But let me tell you what finally happened when I got my groove down. My life changed forever. It was here I found my shine.

One day, after consistently meditating for about two months, I came across a miracle. It was not the kind where Jesus sat in front of me and told me the meaning of life. But it was almost as good. So there I was, doing my daily practice, and I felt myself getting into a deeper state than usual. I began to trust my visualizations as something more powerful than me, but what I found that day changed *everything* about my life.

I found myself seeing a small crack of light. It really was just a sliver, but I had such a profound knowing that there was something special about this light. It wasn't long before this light dragged all of my being into it. Just this very small sliver showed me my deepest, most profound truths. There was such a powerful love radiating from that light. I started to weep with love and appreciation for being alive.

It was then that I *knew* God. It was then that I knew my truth. It was then that I knew my power and that my mission on this earth is to help others see their light. I had always felt a pull to help others, but it was at this very moment that I got a blueprint of my purpose. I got answers to questions I hadn't even yet asked. It was like knowing before I even knew what I needed to know.

Let's just say, I had finally awoken.

Before this experience I had not believed in God. I studied Buddhism to learn how to meditate, but I did not grow up with religion. I didn't feel the need to believe in a being that was so prominent in most religions. I always followed the beat of a different drum, so I figured I didn't need to worship anything to be happy.

But, after this awakening, I had no doubt that the spiritual world is real. I became obsessed in finding out more. I read book after book about near-death experiences and found that even though I didn't die, I felt exactly as those who had faced death and came back to talk about it.

After my experience with the Divine, I started seeing life through different eyes. The grass was greener. The air was fresher. Laughter was louder and my heart smiled brighter. I started living on purpose. I wanted to touch everything, just for the sake of touching it. I wanted to hug tighter. Love bigger. Cry louder. Basically, I wanted to live with childlike joy, and nothing was going to stop me. I was alive. *Finally alive*!

And this was all because I sat my butt down and breathed.

I invite you to take this first step of getting quiet. Schedule some time to close your eyes and be still. I know from experience how hard this can be. Yet that was the first step in finding the most beautiful side of myself. So just trust me when I say that *you will be okay*. You will be loved and safe through this process. You are so much stronger than you think. Your fears have nothing on you!

Meditation doesn't have to be perfect. Many people tell me they can't turn off their brains. That's not the goal of meditation. The goal is to be able to notice all of the chatter in your mind and to not get emotionally attached to it. Your mission when meditating is to simply pay attention to what your thoughts and feelings are, rather than letting them control you.

If you are ready to meditate and dedicate yourself to this practice, your life will change. You will no longer be the person you were before you started meditating. So don't take this practice lightly. My meditation changed *everything* about my life. I am a new and improved version of me. I have finally begun to live in my truth that sat in hiding most of my life.

Meditation doesn't have to be an exact science. The goal is to be consistent and learn to connect with your body. The breath is so important as a centering tool. When we focus on our breathing, we can easily visualize it going in our nose, down our throats, into our lungs, through our bodies, and then back out again.

Thoughts will come. And when they do, just say to yourself, "thinking" and then get back to focusing on your breath. What I also find helpful is to focus on the sensations of your body. How do your hands feel as they rest on your lap? Is your back tight or tense? Is your belly full or hungry? Are your legs falling asleep?

At first you might find these awarenesses distracting. But the beauty of meditation, to me, is that it helps me pay close attention to my entire being. And isn't getting real and present with who you are the goal? That is why I teach paying attention to these parts of yourself so you can begin to see what your body is trying to tell you.

I suggest that you make a goal for yourself to meditate every day, even if for only five minutes. Perhaps you can do this right when you wake up, or right before you go to bed. Some find it helpful to get quiet in the middle of their work day or right before work. Whatever time you choose, try to be consistent and keep going. Like any new habit, it takes time for your body to adjust. You wouldn't go to the gym once and expect to lose ten pounds! Meditation will produce amazing results, but you have to be committed and give it time. And when you do, your life will truly get extraordinary.

I have also found meditation to be far better, and *way* cheaper, than therapy. I'm not knocking therapy. I have had years of therapy—thank you very much—and have learned a lot about myself in the process. But the goal of therapy is to help you dive deep into your emotions so you can clear out what no longer needs to be there. Meditation can be a fast track to your truth.

As a Certified Soul Coach® I am gifted with the opportunity to guide people into a deep meditation and help them connect with their truest selves. I help them see what parts of themselves have been overshadowed by years of shame and fear. Once they get a taste of this truth, they can easily tap into this world that is available to them through meditation. I also help them connect with their spirit guides.

Before my training, I was fortunate enough to connect to this powerful side of myself. I also saw that I am not alone. There is a world of spiritual helpers readily available to give me advice and loving support. This has been the greatest benefit of meditation for me. When I get quiet, I easily connect with my higher self and raise my vibration. I have found a love so great that I'm often brought to tears while meditating.

My trust in the spiritual world has grown tenfold. I have gotten guidance that I would not have thought of on my own. I have healed wounds simply by asking for spiritual guidance. And when I'm meditating, I am able to hear a response. I also get ideas for my teachings. In fact, most of my teachings come from this connection.

I hear all the time about people who use meditation to connect with spirit. In fact there is not a teacher or mentor of mine who doesn't meditate. And if you asked any one of them, I bet they would say meditation changed their lives. Just as you brush your teeth every day to take care of your body, why not make this life-changing tool a part of your daily routine to take care of your soul?

Now have a seat, and breathe. Just breathe.

Exercise

I invite you to try the following meditation as a way to access your inner greatness! This is available as a free guided meditation on my website, along with one on clearing your chakras. I'm more than happy to be your spiritual tour guide.

- Find a quiet place that feels comfortable and soothing, without distractions (yes, including your cell phone).
- Get into a comfortable position, preferably with your spine straight so the energy can flow through your chakras.
- Take some nice deep breaths and notice what those breaths do to your body. Notice how your chest rises and falls. Feel the air go through your nose and visualize it flowing into your lungs, relaxing all that it touches.
- As you continue to watch your breath, imagine and feel all of your body relaxing.
- Then imagine and focus on a beautiful green light around your heart. Imagine this light represents someone who you love deeply. Whether this is a child, a pet, a good friend, or your lover, feel this love and place it into the green light.
- Imagine the green light building into something greater; something bigger. Focus on the loving energy itself, expanded beyond the specific person or pet. It's all pure love.
- Allow this loving green light to grow bigger and begin to cover your entire being. As it does, imagine your body disappearing into this light and becoming one with the light.
- Then imagine this light turning into a brilliant white that extends into the room, your house, your neighborhood, your state, your country, your world.
- As the light grows, realize that you are becoming one with all this light touches. You are radiating a love that is more powerful than words. In this light you also feel the love from others who are connecting their light with yours.

- You have now connected into your divine being. It is here where your truth lies. It is here where your shine has been waiting for you to realize its truth. It is here where you finally remember that all that you are is already perfect. It is here where you know that you are love, and loved more than words can say.

After you spend some time in this truth, begin to wiggle your fingers and toes, do some gentle stretches, take a few deep breaths, and come back to this earthly plane. Know that what you just experienced will change your life forever.

CHAPTER 14

Let Go of Fears

Getting over a painful experience is much like crossing monkey bars.
You have to let go at some point in order to move forward.

C. S. Lewis

One of the benefits of meditation is to help you face your fears. Once I got into the groove of meditation, I used it as my therapy sessions. If I had a problem, I would go to my meditation bench and let the Divine be my therapist (I have come to the point that I easily connect with the Divine in this way). About a year-and-a-half after my divorce, I decided to get really deep with myself and holed myself up in my house for six months. It was during this time that I decided to deal with one of the biggest fears of my life: my emotions!

I used to tell people that my emotions felt so big, I needed a padded room to face them. Have you ever felt that way? Many people tell me that they can't leave a toxic relationship, or quit a miserable job, simply because they are afraid of the emotional consequences of such a decision—either theirs or the other person's. And they are afraid of what life would be like without that person or situation.

But in truth, fear is only False Evidence Appearing Real. What we imagine when we are in fear—the monster in our closets—is not real. As children, our overactive imaginations made us swear up and down that there was a monster in our closet or under our bed. It felt so real at the time that we couldn't sleep and ran into our parents' room to hide in their safety. When fear came knocking at our door, we went running and hiding.

As adults, fear feels much the same. And sadly, while our fears are more sophisticated, they are still only in our heads. Instead of imagining monsters, we are now afraid of ourselves and our own feelings. Worse yet, we become afraid of fear itself.

When I faced my own fear, not only was it a brilliant lesson, I learned that fear has nothing on me. One time, after dealing with the horrible feelings inside of me for over a year-and-a-half after my divorce, I decided to face my demons once and for all. I was tired of being under fear's physical control (my stomach was always bothering me, and I found myself holding my breath a *lot*) and I was ready to cast that feeling off into space!

I had just read the book *Focusing* by Eugene Gendlin. He is a psychotherapist who did research on why some people get better in therapy, while most do not. In his reasearch, the group of people who did get better had a common ability. The ability was that they were able to tap into their bodies to help give them their answers. These people were asked to focus on the sensations in their bodies that were bothering them and name them.

It may seem strange to name a sensation. But with some effort and imagination, I have found this form of therapy to be life changing. When you name a sensation, you inevitably get an answer about what is bothering you and the sensation goes away.

I had just finished Gendlin's book and was determined to find out what this fearful feeling was that had plagued me for so long. I had only ten minutes or so before I had to take my boys to school. I felt strongly, though, that it was now or never. (Due to my tendency to chicken out when it came to dealing with my emotions, when I had a moment of courage, I knew I had to take it.)

I went to my room, closed my eyes, and found the annoying sensation sitting in my belly. I then began the process of naming it. I first thought of what it looked like. It was hard. Round. Covering. Suffocating. Restricting... ah... it lightened up a little. Restricting what? Shame... no. Sadness... no. Love... *yes*! Poof! It was gone! I was restricting love! My body was telling me that my defense mechanism of closing my heart up because I was hurt by my ex-husband was *not* the way to go.

I couldn't believe how fantastic I felt! And it only took ten minutes! But the best lesson of all? I learned to not be so afraid of fear. This monster, this feeling, had plagued me for over a year! By not dealing with it, it only grew bigger and bigger. The sad thing is, I wasn't even aware of what I was afraid of. I just knew it was bad. But in the end, it wasn't nearly as big as I thought it was.

As I did with my childhood monster in the closet, I let my adult feelings grow into imaginary proportions. This is why it is so important to let those ugly buggers out of the closet, put cute tutus on them and perhaps a little lipstick. That fear is only your imagination. So now it's your turn to stop giving it power.

Another powerful way of conquering fear is to get it on paper. When we see our fears, face to face and outside of our own minds, we can then see them for what they are. With our creative imaginations, it's important to bring our fears up to the surface so we can have a little heart-to-heart chat with them.

One of the best ways to do this is to draw out your feelings. You're probably saying to yourself that you're not an artist. What good is a stick figure? But I am not the only one who believes in this therapy, and it helped me get deeper into my feelings and fears than writing about them did.

This technique is used by Dr. Bernie Siegel, best-selling author of *Love, Medicine, and Miracles.* He discovered that by having his patients draw out their feelings about their health, their drawings produced symbols representing their subconscious.

Often our feelings are so deep and internal, we have no idea what is plaguing us. So when we are drawing, we are tapping into the deepest parts of ourselves, which is then brought forth onto paper.

Doing this, I was able to see how disconnected to myself I had become. My feelings began to feel less fearsome and I began to have the courage to face all of my emotions, even when they felt hard and traumatic.

I had become an expert at avoiding my feelings prior to doing this work. If I can heal my fears, so can you. So let's get to work!

Exercise

Time to draw out your fear! Drawing is a powerful way to access your deepest feelings. Don't judge yourself or your work as you do this. This is not an art project. It's an opportunity for your feelings to be heard!

- Get out your crayons, pens, markers, paints, charcoal, or whatever drawing tools suit you. I bought a special book for sketches and some colored pencils, pastels, and artist grade pencils, but those aren't necessary. I also used this exercise as a way to tap into my creative side (but no, I'm not even close to being an artist!).
- If you feel like it, put on some music that fits your mood; music that you feel will support your efforts.
- Then put your drawing tool(s) down on the paper and without thinking, draw. Use colors that fit your emotions. Have at it! Draw out your anger. Draw out your shame. Draw out your sadness. Draw out everything that you feel.

Again, this doesn't have to make sense. The point is to let it all out. And believe me, it will come out. One line at a time.

CHAPTER 15

Harness Your Mind

Whatever the mind can conceive and believe, it can achieve.

Napoleon Hill

One of the benefits of teaching the Law of Attraction (LoA) is that I am constantly learning and growing with my students. I have been teaching about the LoA in various forms every other week for over five years. I have read multiple books, listened to countless YouTube videos, and have gone to numerous seminars on how the LoA works. My all-time favorite teacher is Abraham-Hicks. I have tested and tried all that I learn so I know that what I am presenting has some merit.

Many people who come to my group have heard about the LoA through the book *The Secret* by Rhonda Byrne. Even though this is a good introduction to this amazing way of being, it really only scratches the surface. Before I dive into what this law is really about, let me first tell you how I fell into practicing this life-changing way of thinking.

After being single for about a year-and-a-half, beginning to wake up to who I was, I decided that dating just wasn't for me. I hated the online world and had very little time to meet available guys. I made it a rule for myself that I wouldn't date anyone at work, the gym, or at my boys' school (been there/done that, and found it was not such a good idea). I knew that finding Mr. Right at bars was out of the question, and most of the guys at my church were either married or not to my liking.

At this point I had very little hope of finding a good mate. But then I heard about this "Law of Attraction stuff." I had a friend who had met her soul mate using the LoA. She wrote down what she was looking for, set out the intention that she was going to find him (or that they would find each other) and then went about life with confidence that he was around the corner.

Soon after she set this intention, she was cleaning one of her properties. She owned a house cleaning service, and as the owner, she did not normally do the cleaning herself. But there was no one left to do this particular job and it had to be done that weekend. At the same time that she was at that property, there was a guy who came up from San Diego who was there only on that day to fix some things inside.

They immediately hit it off. It was love at first sight and now they are married and have a baby. She didn't have to go to bars, online chat rooms, or hit on dads at her kid's school. Of course, I liked the idea of my soul mate popping out of nowhere. I mean, if it happened for her, it could happen for me, right?

The funny thing about life is that we are often led to places we don't expect. There seems to be a bigger, grander plan that our minds don't seem able to grasp. After learning about my friend, my sole purpose for using the Law of Attraction was to find my soul mate. But what came to me was so much more.

What I learned with my first experience with the LoA was that by letting go and putting myself in a joyous place, I will attract what is best for me. The most important thing that I can tell you about the LoA is that your life is far greater than you can fathom. And when you live your life consciously and follow the clues, the ride gets extraordinary.

While the LoA is pretty simple, it can feel like you are standing on your head looking at the world upside down. We are taught that in order to be happy we need to get that good job; go to the best schools;

marry the best partner; have perfect little children. We think when we have money, *then* we will be happy. We are sure that if we had the big house up on the hill with the white picket fence, *then* all of our problems will be fixed.

Yet the truth is, our happiness is an inside job. And the Law of Attraction will give you *everything* that you want (and more), as long as you follow some rules. The first rule is that you need to be in a state of joy.

That's a pretty cool thing, right? I mean, who doesn't want to be happy *and* have your cake *and* eat it, too? If you are happy, dreams come true. But somewhere along the line, most of us have picked up the idea that we can only be happy *after* our dreams come true. Somehow we have gotten it backwards! Now you can see why so few of us have what we want.

Therefore, the first step of the Law of Attraction is to be happy *now*!

Now, let's get into the nitty gritty of the LoA. When you want something—I mean really, really want something—you just need to set the intention (i.e., *ask* for it), never doubt that it's coming to you, and then practice being in a place of non-resistance.

According to Abraham-Hicks, if you are feeling good, have no doubts (have no resistance), and are clear about what you want, the Universe will conspire to bring it to you. Our thoughts are the transmitters to this energetic field that will move wherever we direct it to bring what we want to us. Divine timing is a factor (see below). But in general, as long as you're clear, keep your thoughts positive, and stay in a place of receiving, you will get what you ask for.

When I first started practicing the LoA, I had one intention, and that was to find my soul mate. I asked for what I wanted with vision boards. I improved the feng shui of my house so I would be in a good place to receive. But it took over six years to find him. Why did it take so long? Through my own journey, I realized I had a lot of blockages when it came to relationships. One minute I wanted a mate. The next day, not so much. My intention went back and forth; yes and no; okay and *no way, José*. I had been very wishy-washy in what I thought I wanted. Once I became clear about what I wanted and cleared out some blockages, my soul mate did come. And he truly is divine.

Another reason for the delay can be divine timing. Spiritual teacher Matt Kahn speaks in one of his YouTube videos about why many of us aren't receiving our manifestations. He says we must reach a place in our spiritual growth to be prepared and able to receive what we ask for. Once we reach that place, where we are stable and attuned to the Divine, then what we ask for will come.

Think about it this way: if you ask for a million dollars, but still sit in poverty thinking and believe deep down you don't deserve that money, then it won't come to you. But when you raise your self esteem and self worth, and let go of your negative judgments around money, then you are ready to receive. A large part of bringing greatness into our lives is preparing the room so that what is coming can rest and stay a while.

My journey to find my soul mate took a while because I hadn't laid the groundwork to develop who I was meant to become in order to attract him. Yet looking back, the delay was an absolute gift and is one of the main reasons I'm even writing this book. My path was meant to be so much more than to be in a relationship again. A divine plan was unfolding for me one day at a time.

Once I became awakened, I realized that I wanted to inspire people and become a speaker, like my Soul Coaching teacher Denise Linn. I don't really know why, but I have never doubted that this was my path. It was easier for me to manifest these dreams than to manifest a relationship, since I had no blockages in regards to what I wanted. When I read Denise's book *The Soul Loves the Truth*, I knew immediately I had to do this work. Like Denise, I needed to help people find their calling; I needed to help people see their greatness.

The Divine has a plan for you and will bring forth this path as long as you are open and are listening. I manifested so many amazing experiences, and it all started when I opened my mind, listened to my joy, and kept my mind clear of any negative thoughts.

The lesson here? Be mindful of your thoughts. They are powerful. A great book that talks about the power of the Law of Attraction is *E Squared* by Pam Grout. She discusses nine experiments that show how this law works. There are several books about the LoA, but I love how she makes it real by putting it to the test.

I could write my own book about the LoA, since it truly is life changing. I'm very passionate about this way of thinking and have made it my mission to teach any and all people who are willing to listen. But what I have found is that many people are missing the first step in making this law work *for* them and not *against* them. What is missing is their joy. What is missing is the positive thought process that brings more good to their lives. What is missing is the ability to dismantle beliefs that keep most people in a state of resistance.

To help fill in this missing first step, it's important to become aware of your thoughts and understand how they affect *all* that you do. One way you could do this is to keep track, perhaps in a journal if you have one, of any negative thought that goes through your mind over a period of time of your choosing. This is not so that you can find something to judge in yourself, but to help you see the inner conversation that is affecting your life.

I did one experiment where I vowed not to say anything negative for a month. I also vowed that every time I spoke negatively, I would have to restart counting the month. I didn't get very far (maybe two days, and even then I was about to explode with profanities!). I prided myself on being a positive person, but I saw that even I could be dragged down the negative road quite frequently.

In contrast, I did notice that when I was around positive people, in nature or doing something I loved, it was easy to have pure loving thoughts. Do you see the correlation? Whatever is in your environment affects your thoughts. Your thoughts affect the things around you. Those things ultimately affect your life.

So what is the take-home message? Declutter your life. Stop associating with negative people. And surround yourself with people, places, and things that you love. Then watch what greatness comes your way. When you become conscious, the Universe is your best friend, holding your hand, and guiding you every step of the way. But the ball is in your court, my friend. It's time for you to find your joy and stay in a positive state. And when you do, you can move mountains! Or at least the Law of Attraction will make you feel that way.

Exercise

In this exercise, you'll practice setting your intentions. Being in your emotions as you do this is the key to making it work. If you need extra help with this, I offer free guided meditations that you can download from my website to optimize your visualizations.

- Get comfortable and start writing exactly what you want with as much detail as possible. As you write, *feel* how great it would be to have what you want.
- When you are finished writing all the details, close your eyes and bask in the feelings of already having what you want and being what you intend to be.
- Take a moment and send out these intentions to the Universe.
- After you have sent your request, do something to feel good. Pet your cat, play in nature, surround yourself with some amazingly positive people, dance in your kitchen; do *anything* that feels good.

Let go of your request into the ether. It is not your job to figure out *how* you will get this manifestation. Your only job is to feel good. Not a bad job, really. Now you can see why I love the Law of Attraction so much.

CHAPTER 16

Be You, Courageously

Why, sometimes I've believed as many as six impossible things before breakfast.

The Queen, *Alice in Wonderland*

I am one of those crazy people who thrives on being different. I was that four-year-old who wore five skirts at once because I thought it was über fashionable. Then at age thirteen, I dyed my hair black, shaved the sides of my head bald, and whitened my face with baby powder. As a natural redhead, my mom wasn't too excited about this stage. But she did appreciate that I had the courage to stand outside of the crowd and be me.

The funny thing is, I was a very shy kid. If you tried to talk to me, I would run away and retreat to the nearest safe corner. But when it came to my physical appearance, I was willing to stand out and be different. I don't know why this was the case; perhaps it came from being a redhead. But what I do know is that the ability to have the courage to be me has helped me in all areas of my life.

I did not excel in the educational system. I was the youngest of six kids and the *only* one who didn't do sports, get good grades, or do *anything* like my siblings. I swore up and down I was the product of the mailman, or adopted. But I had to admit, I did kind of look like my parents.

So growing up for me was a life spent not fitting in. I was a dancer. I was attracted to the arts. I craved a life of being different, yet felt sad that I didn't fit into my tight-knit family. At age nineteen, I moved away from my hometown of Denver without a plan. I just knew that in order to be me, I had to step away from a life that never felt like me.

Not fitting in was hard. But the pull within me to be authentic was so strong, I had to either connect and embrace this unique me, or risk drowning in my depression. So I chose to leave my comfort zone and see who this Michele really was.

Have you ever been at the point in your life when you just knew you were different, but didn't know how to express it? Or have you ever spent some time following the masses, only to realize that you were miserable and wanted to scream at the top of your lungs *"let me out!!"*? If that is you, I want to first congratulate you for connecting to your truest authentic self. The fact that you have even questioned your existence says that you are on the road to connecting to your truth. The bottom line is that when you find your truest self, you'll begin to realize that you are completely unique and extraordinary.

When you tap into your greatness, you will find that fitting in was *never* an option. You see, we are all unique, but we live in a society that encourages conformity. It takes courage and strength to reach a place of the unknown. In fact, when we do, others around us will do whatever it takes to keep us in alignment with *their* beliefs.

Being different as a kid is a recipe for being picked on or bullied. The kids who dress differently, or who have different skin or hair, or who are in any other way considered "not normal," are chastised simply because those around them are uncomfortable. Why is that? Let's look at the complexities of the collective consciousness.

As I've said before, we are all made up of energy. This energy, as proven by quantum physics, is as real as the chair you are sitting on. Each of us is radiating an energetic "vibe," so to speak, with all of our emotions and thoughts. The person next to you emits a vibration too, which, if it's similar to yours (i.e., similar thoughts, similar beliefs), will feel comfortable to be around, since it is familiar.

Like attracts like for a good reason. The universal energy that is within us pulls us all together so we are more equipped to navigate our world. We are similar to waves in the ocean, which are created when one particle of water moves and the rest move in the same rhythmic pattern. This pull seems comfortable and natural, so it makes sense to follow along.

As humans, we exist in a sea of movement, like those waves, and when the majority is pulling the energy one way, it seems easier to just follow along. The only problem is that when the people around you are swimming in very rough waters, it can be very hard to pull yourself out.

Say you decide to get on a boat and paddle to safety. The waves try to pull you back with so much might and strength that you find your boat capsizing, perhaps several times. But with determination, you keep paddling. You keep rowing as if your life depended on it. Pretty soon, you can see a beautiful island full of people who had already made that journey. And once you get closer, they pull you in with ease. At that point, you can let go of the paddle and finally let the current bring you to where you were meant to be.

This is the analogy that many of us face. We are stuck in a world of negativity and suffering. The sea of people around us wants to keep us down, but it is our job to fight the current. It is our God-given right to coast up to our island of greatness and be the best that we are meant to be.

This island represents our spiritual pull. When we are in its waters, life feels smooth and peaceful. It is here where we can be whoever we want to be. You can have crazy hair. You can walk on stilts, juggling four balls while playing the harmonica. You can start a dance party in the middle of a parking lot. You can start a television show about gardening naked (aren't naked shows the thing now?).

The point is, when you get out of the grasp of all the negative energy that is gathered around you, you can begin the journey of finding your own uniqueness. When you start to live a fearless life of,

"I don't care what others think of me," then you are onto something good. You will start to emit a powerful energy that will attract the kind of people who are similar to you (remember, like attracts like).

When I started to embrace my uniqueness and follow this internal guidance, I opened up to a whole new world. I made more friends than I could count, and I found myself meeting others who were as courageous and passionate about life as I was.

When I started my soul's journey, I set the intention of finding like-minded people. This came quickly with my Law of Attraction group, and I was excited to be that resource for others to find their tribe as well. In fact, I had made a space for others to join in who were looking for the exact same thing. I became a lighthouse for others who wanted to know their truth. And together, we have developed an amazing community.

Our energy is powerful, which is why I believe we have grown so fast. Our collective consciousness is one that embraces growth and personal development. But most importantly, we embrace each other's uniqueness.

Now, if you're living in a world where there is no one who thinks like you or there are people trying to bring you down, there is hope. There is *always* hope. But the first thing you need to do is to connect with your beautifully unique self. Stop listening to those around you and find the courage and strength to get out of the rough waters and onto the boat of your truth.

This journey may not be easy. But it is so worth it! Never fear, my friend. I have a belief in you that you can and *will* arrive on your island of bliss. The first step, though, is to commit to this ride. You need to say "*Yes*! I am ready to shine!" And be the most exceptional you that you can be. Because you are, in fact, the only *you* there is.

So repeat after me (yes, out loud!), "I am amazing! I have a greatness inside that is longing to come out. I will do whatever it takes to be authentically me. The world is ready for me. I am ready to be all that I was meant to be. So *watch out world! Here I come*!"

Exercise

This is an exercise in courage. Imagine yourself as if you are a child with no fear or sense of limitation. Anything goes. As an example, when my brother and I were young, we thought we could dig our way to China. So guess what we did? We started digging! Let's start digging...

- Write a list of all the "crazy" things that you have thought about doing. Call it your "Bucket List of Possibilities." Don't hold back what you write.
- When you finish your list, put stars next to the things that you know you definitely want to do.
- At the bottom of the list write, "I am setting my intention to do all the starred items on this list by the end of this year."
- Then sign it, date it, and put it in a place where you can see it every day.

This exercise will open up *so* much for you! I guarantee it. I wrote my own bucket list of possibilities and achieved all that I put on my list, including skinny dipping in the moonlight of a lake just outside of the city. It was exhilarating and kept me "high" for a long time. It also taught me to be courageous. And let me tell you, having courage has gotten me far. How else do you think I'm writing this book?

Shine on, my friends. Your magnificently unique self is waiting.

CHAPTER 17

Step out of Comfort

If you want to grow a muscle, you must lift something out of your comfort zone. Push beyond what is comfortable, if you don't there will be no growth.

Tony Robbins

The previous chapter prepared you for this next step to finding your shine. In order to reach farther, we need to first dip our toes in the water. How many of you dive right into a freezing cold body of water? Most of us need a little warm-up. We need to take baby steps. I don't advocate diving into the deep end until you at least know how to swim. That's why the last exercise is so important: it's meant to help you be prepared to reach a little farther and step outside of your comfort zone. So if you haven't done that exercise already, I highly encourage you to take a step back and do it. It's simple and fun!

When I look back at my life, I can see now how each step I took was necessary to lead me to the next. I tried meditation, which was uncomfortable at first, but eventually I got the hang of it. I read books before I went to seminars. I signed up with trainings before I started my own practice. I watched hours of motivational speakers before I got on stage.

It's been a step-by-step process that has led me to the point where I'm ready to dive into that vast pool of courageousness. I have learned to be brave reaching outside of my comfort zone. I have taken action steps that have made me feel like I was going to vomit at times, but I have come to accept that reaching outside of one's comfort zone isn't always comfortable.

I once heard transformational speaker and self-help goddess Lisa Nichols say, "If your dreams don't scare you, they're not big enough." Reaching a place of uncertainty is scary. But that doesn't mean you shouldn't go for it. Think about the times throughout your life when you have reached outside of your comfort zone. Do you remember the feelings you had when you moved through the fear to the other side? Do you ever regret doing what scared you so much?

Think back to that first game you were in, feeling insecure and awkward. Think about the times when you started a new job, learning new skills. I remember being a new nurse and having panic attacks every day before I went to work for at least the first six months. There's nothing at all comfortable about savings someone's life when you are still learning how to do it! What if you went to a party where you didn't know anyone but you ended up meeting your soul mate there? What if you hadn't gone? It certainly was worth moving through your nervousness and fear, right?

You see, life is full of firsts and times of discomfort. And every one of them scared you. Why? Because it was uncomfortable; it was out of your comfort zone. The best part of being outside of your comfort zone is moving into your growth zone. How cool is that?

Have you ever thought to yourself, "My life is boring," or "Nothing exciting ever happens to me"? These thoughts tend to come up when you have played it safe for too long. Most of us crave excitement, but unfortunately, most of this comes from negative energy. Why else do you think the news is all about trauma, car chases, and political scandal? It's because it gets us out of our boring lives.

A far better and more productive way to get some action is to do something different. Just the feeling of being uncomfortable will stir some growth inside of you. It will make you feel alive and recharged. So I encourage you to fight your way past the fear of "No way, José, that's too scary!" Instead, start saying, "What else is possible?" or "Why not?"

Take a deep breath, put on your magic cape, don some protective gloves—whatever you need to do to try something completely out of your comfort zone—and you will connect with a part of you that has been wanting to come out and play for a very long time.

One of my favorite pieces of advice on stepping out of your comfort zone is in the dating books that I have read. Many of them say that in order to find your soul mate you need to look in places that you never frequent. Often our soul mate is very different from us and can help us grow and become our best selves. We grow best when we are challenged by what we eventually overcome and/or endure. So it's no accident that the person who is a perfect match for us often seems like the opposite.

Another positive aspect of reaching outside of your comfort zone is the courage it gives you in all areas of your life. I try to do something new every day. Even if it's taking a new route to work or doing a video blog, I gain confidence by just doing it. For me, no matter what "it" is, as long as it's different, I feel it will benefit me in more ways than one.

I have become a "yes woman." I listen to my intuition and say yes, especially when it scares me. The more a major life decision scares you, chances are the more you need to do it. I'm constantly reminding myself that stepping out of my comfort zone is leading me to my growth zone. And being scared is just part of the process, not a warning to stay away.

Think of the last time you did something that was scary and completely uncomfortable. Then ask yourself two questions: 1) Did I survive it? and 2) What were the rewards? The next time you are faced with such a situation, and as long as you're not putting your life or someone else's life at risk, ask yourself what the worst thing that might happen would be. If the answer isn't death, than I think you should give it a whirl!

When it comes to connecting to your truest self, this is a very important step to take if you are committed to finding your shine. Very often, our shine is found simply by trying new things. I used to tell my friends when I took cello lessons that I was sure I had a hidden talent that was dying to come out. If I had never tried to play the cello, I would not have known how much I enjoyed it. And now I know that trying it out helped me to learn more about my interests and my passions, and that playing cello is something I could always do again if I chose to put the time into it.

Suppose your shine is to run a business and be an entrepreneur. If you never try doing it, you'll never discover this about yourself. The first step is to take the first step, no matter how uncomfortable it is. And practice makes perfect, so start now by reaching outside of your comfort zone in all that you do. Then don't be hard on yourself for something you don't know. We are all beginners in every new thing we try.

I look back at my life and see how each courageous step was what has led me to my true path. Taking the risk to become a Certified Soul Coach®, even though I felt completely inept, was a necessary step to finding my passion. When I went to the training in San Luis Obispo, California, I sat in my hotel room the day before the training was to start, trying to talk myself out of a panic attack.

My ego was telling me that I was a fraud and that I had no right to be there. It kept telling me to make excuses to go home. It was better (it said) to save face than to show up with all of these other, far superior people who were *really* ready to take on this intensive training. Have you ever heard that voice? Once I got there I found that each and every one of my fellow students had the same feelings as I did. They quickly became my soul family, and that training has been one of the most life-changing things I've ever done.

Then there was the time I took over the Law of Attraction group, knowing that by doing so, I had to actually get in front of people and teach, in spite of never having taught a class in my life. Had I not pushed through my discomfort around the decision I made to take on the class, I never would have known that my life's path was to teach and inspire.

All of the great things in life are just outside of your comfort zone. Your shine will begin to get brighter and surer with each uncomfortable step you take. You will then participate in more opportunities that will help you grow into the best you that you can be. Your shine will make you courageous even when you're scared. But you have to take those first steps, no matter how much they scare you.

Think about this scenario for a minute: You walk into a room full of people you don't know. You are nervous because it is an event where there are people who (your ego is telling you) are better, wiser, cooler then you are. Everyone seems to be comfortable and sure of themselves. You swear you are the only one with toilet paper on your shoe and food in your teeth (even if that were true, it's not the truth of the real you!).

You then take a deep breath and remind yourself that you are bad ass (yes you are!) and you begin to talk to the woman standing next to you. It just so happens that she owns a publishing company, and after a brief conversation with you, she gives you her card and says she would love to check out your book. Then, with this newfound confidence, you move on to a man nearby and strike up a courageous conversation (because it does get easier, although still a little uncomfortable). You find out that he is looking for someone to be on his radio show.

At this point you are beaming with joy. At the end of the event, you walk out, get in your car, and see a text from someone you met recently at a seminar. They want you to speak at their next conference. You have never really spoken on stage and your initial reaction is to run away and say, "Hell no!" But given your good momentum, you say "Yes!" Can you imagine the doors that are swinging open now?

This is how important getting out of our comfort zone is. The Universe will provide for us, but we need to get out of our own way. We need to say "Yes" even when we feel like saying "No." We need to reach farther and farther each time, so our muscles will stay fit. We need to keep taking steps forward, no matter how much it scares us.

When I was in the seventh grade, I auditioned for the all-school Denver Public Schools summer play of Annie. I had recently found my passion in dancing, but did not have the ability to act or sing. I sat with my mom in the auditorium, trying to figure out a way of getting out of the audition. I concocted a plan in which I would say that I needed to go to the bathroom and then I'd high-tail it for the back door. Then I thought I could fake a seizure. Or better yet, I could fake my death! Luckily, my mom—the loving intuitive woman that she is— did not let me follow through with any of these plans. And when my name was called, instead of running for the exit, I got on stage and faced my fear.

Was I picked as Annie? Um, no. But I did get a part in the chorus and had the time of my life! And my biggest lesson was that because I pushed through the discomfort, I grew from the experience. I have often thought about that shy seventh grader, who was too scared to speak to her neighbors when it came time to ask for the money for Girl Scout cookies, yet still got up on stage and sang courageously.

Think back to the times in your life when you enlisted your own courage. Each of those experiences can serve as constant reminders that you can keep on stepping out of your comfort zone. Remember... you never gave up on learning how to walk!

Exercise

This exercise is about practicing to say "Yes!"
- Make a list of things you have been wanting to do but have put off.
- Try to do something new every day, even if it's driving a different way to work or trying a new machine at the gym.
- Include things on this list that seem completely out of your reach and put stars by them.
- Take the starred items and set the intention of doing them.

- Tell a friend who will hold you accountable, and do whatever it takes to do what you've said you're going to do.

I guarantee that your life will change when you do this exercise. Who knows who you will meet? Who knows what talents, gifts, and passions will arise when you decide to say "*Yes!*"

CHAPTER 18

Create Miracles

Seek not to change the world, but choose to change your mind about the world.

A Course in Miracles

A *Course in Miracles* is a spiritual practice that has changed millions of lives. I have integrated its philosophy into my life and it has, in fact, produced miracles for me. And fast. What it teaches is that anything can change in a heartbeat, if you choose to see it in a different light. When you do, that is your miracle. In her number one bestseller *A Return to Love*, spiritual icon Marianne Williamson offers us the truth about love and life. So often we think suffering is our birthright. We think the world outside of us is out to get us. We think things in nature, the economy, our neighbors, are designed to sabotage our lives.

But when we look at it, and life, from a different vantage point, as *A Course in Miracles* teaches, we see our unhappiness is really from our disconnect from the divine nature within ourselves. Her book shows us that the love we seek is not from the outside world, but is bursting within our truest beings. And when tapped into, everything in our world changes in an instant.

There is not a single thing that doesn't have a different side. For example, the tragedies of the world can be looked upon as a blessing.

One example is the September 11 attacks. I'm not saying the event was a blessing, but the love that came forth and brought people together because of it was truly the miracle. *Meetup* (the online social networking portal that brings people together offline) came about because of this event. As of the writing of this book, it has over thirty-two million members in over 180 countries and helps people connect in the flesh. So many people live lonely lives and don't know how to connect with others. *Meetup* helps fill that gap and helps to create friendships and relationships that might not have otherwise happened.

Another example is the Sandy Hook Elementary School shooting in Newtown, Connecticut in 2012, where twenty children were killed. Having kids similar in age to those poor children who died, I couldn't even watch the news without retching in pain. Then I went to a service at the Unity church in Portland, Oregon where Reverend Lisa Davis gave the most powerful talk about this tragedy.

At first I thought I would have to leave, because I couldn't even listen in fear I would fall apart in pain. Yet it was the most beautiful service I had ever heard. She spoke about how these children did not die in vain. Instead, families from all over the world were now embracing their children and giving them the love and attention that they deserved. People began to play with their children, when the day before they were glued to their computer or busy focusing on their jobs. We all held on to our loved ones, young or old, as if we would never see them again. The love that burst forth was a gift those little children bestowed upon us. In fact, Marianne Williamson spoke publicly about how the loving embraces felt around the globe was the miracle.

There was not a dry eye that day, and for the first time I saw that the miracles that occur in our lives can happen in an instant. It's all about how we see things and allowing a deeper, more loving perspective to come through.

Every situation has both what is *not* wanted and what *is*. With each bad, a desire of what is wanted is birthed, and then it is our job to focus on the desire instead of on what is not wanted. My favorite teacher who speaks about this frequently is Abraham-Hicks. Abraham teaches that when we are in a situation that produces a negative feeling or doubt, the flip side is an even stronger version of what we do want.

So often we live our lives unconsciously, not taking the time to decipher what our desires are. But looking more closely, it can be seen that bad or negative situations shoot rockets of desire into our consciousness, simply because of this contrast. This contrast is then showing us more of what we do want. And that, my friend, is the miracle.

For example, if you are in a job you hate, you have a difficult boss, are underpaid, and are exhausted every day when you finally make it home, what is the first thing on your mind? "I want something better!" The way you perceive your situation is what gets you the new job that pays better, that you love, and gives you the opportunity to work with people who inspire you. How you do this is to bless the contrast, and then focus on what you want instead. In fact, words of appreciation will lead you closer to what you want, simply because you are in a state of no resistance.

Life is filled with contrast, and you can choose how you perceive each moment. When something "bad" happens, you can choose to be the victim and shout out to the world how unfair everything is (which will only get you more of what you don't want). Or you can choose to be thankful that this event is showing you the clarity of what you really, deeply want (which will cause you to draw more of that into your life). This work can be just as effective with events that have already happened.

For many of us, our pasts are the ball and chain that prevents us from developing into who we truly are. We speak the same old story, revisit memory lane over and over again, and then wonder why we never grow past these negative beliefs.

My "poor-me book" was filled with facts that I decorated, colored, laminated, and photocopied. Then I delivered them to everyone's inbox. I saw my past as permanent and unchangeable. These events had created my life, and by God, I was going to get pleasure out of milking these stories for all that they were worth.

It wasn't until my Soul Coaching training that I was given the permission to stop these stories and see them from a different perspective. The interesting thing about our past is that they carry energy that gets stuck; our negative feedback loop is its fuel. So when I dared to speak a different, more positive story, I shifted this energy. I felt blessed by my past and no longer felt that it was a curse.

Then everything changed. I mean everything. I took any and all situations and saw the advantage. My upbringing with a single mom who had very little time for me was the sore subject that brought me a lot of pain. Then I began to see that because of this situation, I was able to be independent and resilient. I have always been able to care for myself. And even though my mom didn't have enough time (she had six kids, for Christ's sake!), she showed all of my siblings and me that she respected and trusted us to make the right decisions. I'm proud to say we all turned out well.

If you feel stuck in a story, it's time to find appreciation for what has happened and thank the contrast that has burst forth to show you more of what you do want. This can be done with your past and with *every* situation that comes your way. When you do this work, you will never feel like a victim again. Your miracle is waiting...

Exercise

Here's how to produce a miracle. The point of this exercise is to produce a visual representation of your life and pay attention to your emotions as you see your life revealed on paper. It's time to let go of the past.

- Draw a timeline of your life. You can do this in whatever way feels right. It can be a straight line, a tree of life, or even a spreadsheet on your computer. Get creative and pull out your paints, crayons, or colored pencils (pixels!).

- On your timeline, write a brief description of the major or memorable events of your life.
- When you are finished writing about these events, go to the ones that were difficult. Think about the contrast between your negative story of each one and what you wish would have happened. Find appreciation for each event, even if all you can get out of it was that you survived and you now appreciate that you are so bad ass you can survive anything!
- Write down these words of appreciation and make them bold and colorful.
- Then cross out, color over, or paste something on top of the negative events in your life.
- At this point, you should only be able to see your words of appreciation. If you so desire, start a new timeline displaying this positive new version of your life.

When you are done, take a deep breath, put your hand on your heart and say (out loud) the words, "I am a powerful being. I'm so thankful for being able to see the contrasts that help me bring more of what I do want into my life!"

CHAPTER 19

Be Joyful

Joy is prayer; joy is strength; joy is love;
joy is a net of love in which you can catch souls.

Mother Teresa

One of my favorite things about the Law of Attraction is that it works best if you are in a state of joy. I love that my group is called the Law of Attraction for Happiness, because I truly believe that when we practice this law, we realize that being happy is *all* we have to do.

Those of you who have studied the LoA may think I'm crazy to say this. We are told we need to do our vision boards, create visualizations, say our affirmations, and that by doing so, what we want will come to us. This is true. But manifesting also depends on how high our vibration is. And the quickest way to raise our vibration is to be in a state of joy. In fact, my entire Happiness Coaching training could have been narrowed down to one short question: "What does joy ask of you to do today?" That's it!

The Universe has an intelligence that we take for granted. Our only job is to launch our desires into the ether and then be in a place of receptivity. This goes for finding our inner shine, too. In fact, the easiest way to find your shine is to ask yourself every day when you wake up, "What does joy ask of me today?". Then do it! Your joy will lead the way.

Here's something to think about: Say you are in the company of two people. One is grumpy, defensive, sad, and feels hopeless. The other person is beaming with joy, smiling, making eye contact with you, and has a friendly demeanor. Wouldn't you want to hang out with the happy person?

Now, let's pretend you are the Universe (because you *are* very powerful!) and you get to choose who will get the magic prize of abundance. I bet if you handed the prize to the guy who was grumpy, he would question your motives and wonder what's in it for *you*. The happy guy, on the other hand, would gladly accept it without questions.

That is how the Universe works. When we are in receptive mode, all greatness comes to us, and often very quickly. The hard part is getting into the mode of letting it in. That is why joy comes in so handy.

Here's a little experiment to try: Just try thinking of something that makes you incredibly happy. I often do this with my patients, and even when they are in pain, they can usually think of one thing that makes them happy. It could be a pet or your child, perhaps a beautiful place you have visited, or maybe a memory of a time in your life when you felt blissfully happy. For me, I always think of snuggling with my boys. I feel so much joy having them in my arms, and the love I feel is so strong it puts me in a perfect place of joy.

Once you get this happy thought front and center, pay attention to your body. How does it feel? Is it light? Is your breathing calm? Do you feel relaxed and soft? Isn't it wonderful to feel so good?

The best part of this is that by being in this blissful state, you are now in a receptive mode and your vibration is high as a kite. That rocket of desire was already placed in your vibrational escrow. So now your job is simply to be happy. You can't beat that!

You may be wondering, "How *can* I be happy?" Many of you may say, "The world is filled with suffering. How can I be happy when so many people aren't?" Or maybe you tell yourself that there is nothing to be happy about, that life has been more than unfair to you.

One thing I love about my nursing career is that I see people who have nothing, but still act as if they have everything. I had a patient who was accidentally shot in the face during a hunting excursion when he was nineteen years old. He became a quadriplegic and had to use a voice box to communicate, since he had no vocal cords.

I met him when he was forty-five. He had lived all those years in complete dependence on others. He needed to be turned every two hours to prevent bedsores. He needed to be bathed, cleaned, and fed by his family, who had been doing this for over twenty-five years. Yet when I met him, I couldn't get over how happy he was. His smile lit up the room. He would love to joke with me and the other nurses and got great pleasure in sharing his life with whoever came into his room. I remember feeding him and thinking to myself, "How is it that this guy is happier than almost anyone I have met?" He inspired me to understand the truth about joy.

Joy is not about having a fancy car, big house, or high paying job. Joy is not about making millions, having lots of fancy possessions, or wearing big diamond rings. Joy is about love. Joy is about the small pleasures in life. Joy is a mental state of gratitude for all that you have. My joy is laughing with my kids. My joy is walking in the forest by my house and listening to the creek flow by. My joy is hearing the crunch of the earth below my feet and smelling the pine trees breeze past my nose.

That is my joy. And when I'm in this state, all of my clarity, creativity, and productivity come easy. Life should be easy. But we are often in a place where we feel that we need to figure out the magic formula in order to be happy. That magic is joy. Pure and simple. We don't need to figure out how it will work. That is Spirit's job. I am not alone in this belief. If you ask any great teacher in the world, they will tell you that the *how* is not important. What is important is the *why*. Your job is to do whatever it takes to be in a joyful state so that your *why* can be *realized*.

If you are reading this book, I'm sure you are asking yourself,

"Why am I here? What is my purpose?" The question to also ask yourself is, "Why is this thing that brings me joy so important?" If it feels good, then you are on to something. If it feels bad, then it's time to let that thing go or give no attention to it.

We each have something in ourselves or in our lives that brings us joy. For some, programming computers brings them joy. For others, it's being around children and helping them shine. For me, I experience deep joy when I inspire others, and I also find tremendous joy in writing. Even writing this book now is one of the most joyful things I have ever done.

So what brings *you* joy and why is it important to you? What makes you feel unstoppable? What books are you drawn to in a bookstore? What types of activities make you want to jump for joy? What in your life makes you feel alive and by doing that activity you lose track of time?

Our joy is a gift to help us to navigate our truth. And at the same time, our joy is what brings more greatness into our lives. I don't know why more of us aren't taught to just focus on our joy instead of groveling through life for a paycheck.

Our joy will provide clarity for what will bring us more money. We all know that worrying about money does no good. So why not set the intention of having more money, shoot that desire into the ether, than be in a joyfully receptive mode to receive? For most, this may seem too good to be true. But it has worked time and time again for the most successful people in life.

Let's take Steve Jobs, the founder of Apple, as an example. Steve had a passion for his dream. He had a passion for his products, and whenever he spoke about them, you could tell he was in his place of joy. I'm sure at times he may have felt defeated. He *did* actually get fired from his own company at one point. But when he came back, he did what he did best, and that was creating joyfully what he loved. It was his shine, combined with his joy, that made him so successful.

This is the simple truth for you, too. Your joy will guide you, sustain you, and bring to you all that you desire. That is why it is so important to practice joy daily.

So starting today, ask yourself that very important question, "What does joy ask of me today?" Keep a journal and write down the things that bring you joy. After a while, you will begin to see a pattern. You will also start seeing more and more great things coming your way, and they will open even more doors and opportunities for you.

See every situation as an opportunity to grow and discover more of who you are. If the thing you are doing makes you feel heavy, change the channel. If it makes you feel good, stay there for a bit. Bask in that joy. Let the lightness of the situation lift you further. By doing so, you also prolong your ability to be in your high-flying place where your vibrational escrow is eager to be a match to your human reality.

I know this may all seem counterintuitive. We are taught that life is hard, and that with a little bit of blood and sweat, then we will achieve our goals. We are told, "No pain, no gain." Well I'm here to tell you that those old, outdated beliefs need to be thrown in the garbage. They need to be shot off into outer space. They need to be erased from your memory.

Repeat after me... "All I need to do is be in joy." Then follow up with, "What does joy ask of me today?" Then *do it*! Now that you have clarified what you want, it's your turn to step through the open door. There's no point in having a doorway if you are unwilling to walk through it. But you have to move. You have to take action.

Exercise

Practice being in joy!

- Write a list of *all* of the things that bring you joy. Set a timer for five minutes and keep writing. Be creative and don't leave anything out.
- As joy asks of you, start doing these things!

One time I was in a funk and I asked what joy wanted me to do that day. I heard, "Go play with a hula hoop." So that is exactly what I did. In fact, by doing so, I was inspired to do a class on having fun and bringing out your inner child. I got everyone a hula hoop and we all got to be a kid again. Some of my students told me that they were so inspired by the hula hooping, they took the same idea to a group they were teaching and it was a huge hit!

That is what happens when you follow joy. Greatness steadily comes your way.

Be Happy for No Reason

Have you ever had those moments when you were happy just because? Have you been happy when there was absolutely nothing happening in your world to produce this happiness? I've had those blissful moments that made me giggle with excitement. I've felt so alive and so content with sitting exactly where I was sitting, and yet I couldn't tell you what had gotten into me.

This happened to me recently after I saw spiritual teacher Matt Kahn. The interesting thing about Matt is that his teachings are so deep and mind blowing, our physical minds have a hard time grasping them. The last time I saw him speak, I could barely stay awake. I remember thinking it was rather rude of me to fall asleep. I avoided eye contact with him. Even though there were hundreds of us there, I worried that he would scowl at me for falling asleep. He is not that kind of guy—in fact, he is the most loving being I have ever met—but my guilt and shame for falling asleep produced these stories. At the end of his talk, Matt commented that what was shared was incredibly deep, so it would take time for us to fully absorb it. I decided that my conscious mind had to fall asleep so my subconscious could understand better.

The next day, though, I was completely blissed out. There was nothing in my world that had increased my joy. Really, I had fallen into my natural state and felt giddy to be alive. I was truly happy for no reason.

Our natural state is one of joy. We often forget this, though, so providing ourselves the much-needed reminder can bring us back to this state. When I am in my truth, I float into this blissful world and no one can take me out of it. I feel completely in the flow and smile at all the beauty around me. Another way of reaching this, besides listening to Matt Kahn, who I highly recommend, is to practice mindfulness.

Soon after a breakup from a guy with whom I shared a deep connection, I retreated to my meditation bench for solace. I had not meditated much since I had met him and I knew it was time to reconnect with Source energy. As I sat there, I was inspired to practice mindfulness the rest of the day. I knew I couldn't change the past, and I was too hurt to think of the future. Therefore, all I had was that moment. And it was time to pay attention.

After I was done meditating, I had what I call a spiritual orgasm. Yes, that's what I said. Orgasm. Let's just say it's a kind of bliss to the nth degree. And it happened fast. After I got up from my meditation bench, I focused on everything that I looked at and asked myself, "What is that?" Like a two-year-old, I was living in a world that seemed new and magical. I touched everything. I felt the texture of the walls, my clothes, my skin. I noticed how things smelled, and I even tasted the air as it entered my mouth.

I went down to my kitchen sink and sat in awe as I watched the water come from the faucet and warm my hands. Then I looked at my hands and began to cry. Not out of sadness, but out of pure joy that my hands were so beautiful. They were functional and moved about as I asked them to. My skin was perfectly intact and I cried tears of joy for how beautifully my body worked for me. It was almost like I had never paid attention to the complexities of my hands, and my body was thanking me for paying attention.

Then I went for a walk and wanted to yell out to everyone in the world to open their eyes to all of the beauty that I was seeing: the contrasting colors; the sounds of the birds; the leaves blowing cheerfully in the breeze. I laughed out loud like a child would when seeing something new and exciting. I had seen these objects thousands of times before, but this was the first time that I was truly present and awake to see it in all its infinite detail. I was happier than I had ever been. And it was for no reason at all except that I was alive.

I had an awareness soon after this that helped me put this experience into perspective. When thinking about the spiritual world, our souls exist as pure love and are connected to everything. We come down to this earthly plane and want to experience something different. So the one big difference, I believe, is that on Earth, we can experience life through our five senses. We have the opportunity to experience life with our human bodies, and in return we light up our spiritual selves with the kind of giddiness I experienced that day.

That is why so many people speak of mindfulness. To be completely present is our gift to our spiritual selves. That is where the truth lies. Yesterday is merely a fantasy in our heads, since it no longer exists. Tomorrow is also a made-up world and is often the cause of our anxiety. But today, we are breathing. We are seeing. We are tasting, touching, hearing.

I have done groups where we went on a mindfulness walk, tuned into our senses, and paid attention to all that we saw. We walked in silence, asking ourselves the question "What's that?" with childlike wonder. Afterwards, each one of us shared what we noticed most. What was fantastic was how happy people were after that short walk. They each saw something different, yet they all collectively felt joyful and at peace. Most were happy for no reason except that they were alive and had opened their eyes to the beauty that was right in front of them.

This is the beauty of meditation and why I'm a strong advocate of meditating. When you meditate, you learn to quiet your mind, or at the very least, learn to keep your thoughts from distracting you. Then you can learn to be fully present. And by doing so, you realize that there is nothing keeping you from being happy. The trees, the birds, the breeze... those are the things that will awaken your spirit. But you have to wake up to your now. Your present is your present.

Exercise

Let's go on a mindfulness walk. The first step is to get in touch with your senses.

- Take a moment to close your eyes and awaken your body.
- Focus on your eyes for a minute and imagine that your eyes are seeing with a superpower, like Superman.
- Move your attention to your ears and imagine them being able to hear everything, like our furry best friends who raise their ears when a pin drops.
- Next, move your focus to your hands and pay attention to what they are touching. Ask yourself, "How does this feel?" with everything you touch.
- Next, pay attention to your mouth and tongue. Can you taste anything? Is it warm or are you feeling cool air flow through?
- Finally, what do you smell? Is it a good smell or bad smell? Can you guess what you are smelling?
- After you get in touch with your senses, go outside and play the "What's that?" game. Focus on each of your five senses and really *notice* what you notice. What do you see and hear? What colors are being shown to you right in front of your face? Notice the contrast of the ground compared to the tree or house and how they feel different. What do you taste and smell? Pay attention to *everything*.

When you are finished, take a deep breath and give thanks for that beautiful moment of presence. What a gift you just gave your spirit!

Now What?

It's About the Journey

Write it in your heart that every day is the best day in the year.

Ralph Waldo Emerson

Imagine that you are in a movie. This can be a comedy or a romance. Perhaps it's an adventure with Indiana Jones-type experiences. Or maybe it's science fiction and you get to play with really cool technology. You can add characters throughout the story and take them out as you please. You can move the drama and story in any way you like. The music can bring tears of joy or help a broken heart mend. You are the director, so whatever you choose, this is your movie.

In truth, your *life* is your movie. My eleven-year-old son once told me he feels like his life is a movie. He said this with a big smile on his face and his headphones on. I, too, feel like I'm in a movie and often feel giddy thinking about the opportunities available in this adventure we call life. I often feel like we come into this life simply to make our movie. And when it's over, we leave the theater of this life and go to the next one.

Life is a journey that is meant to be fun. We often take life too seriously and then realize when it's too late that we rarely played. Many of us are stuck in the past, reliving a memory that is no longer real. Or we fuss about the future and waste the majority of our lives worrying about something bad that may never happen.

But if we lived in the now and thought of life as a movie, we would enjoy it more. We would look at our future as an exciting adventure and would eagerly anticipate everything that manifests. Our days are the reels of film that keep on playing forward, allowing us to experience more and more. There is nothing we need to do but enjoy the ride.

What would your life look like if you followed your joy more? Every moment you could ask yourself, "What's next?". What if you said *Yes* when your heart called out to you? What if you trusted divine guidance and let go of things you had no control over?

What if you breathed consciously and opened your eyes to a world filled with beautiful colors and smiling faces? This world would reflect to you exactly how you feel. What if each experience brought you closer to a life of bliss, and the tragedies were no longer that bad?

What if you lived your life just for the fun of it? Imagine the possibilities of life simply because it feels good. Let go of those things in your life that step on your buzz of positivity. And laugh more. Laugh louder. Laugh for no reason at all.

Because that is why you are here, my friend. You're not here to impress anyone or earn anyone's love. You are here to love and be loved just as you are. You are here to grow and create whatever you allow to come through you. You are given the ability to use your mind, and the only thing that keeps you from living fully is you.

One year on Thanksgiving I was coming home from a friend's house early in the morning. I was feeling out of sorts and sad about a relationship in my life that wasn't working out. As I was driving, it finally hit me. I was okay. As I crossed a bridge over the Columbia River and saw the sunrise behind beautiful snow-capped Mount Hood, and a full moon setting over the river on the opposite side, I knew in that moment that I was perfect.

I needed nothing else than *this* moment. I was a spiritual being experiencing a human life. And what a ride it has been! My breath was my connection to the Source energy that produces worlds. I just had to breathe to remember this. In that moment, I knew that my life was a fantastic journey and everything I was going through was simply an experience.

I remembered in that moment as I drove across this bridge that my connection with the Divine and my truth was my greatest gift to myself. I realized that every "bad" circumstance in my life was a divine orchestration that would help me manifest my greatest self.

I realized that love is our natural way of being and that each and every one of us deserves to be loved equally. I thought of all my patients who had passed on, and smiled as I remembered how much they touched my life. I reminisced about the conversations I had with my spiritual teachers and mentors, and finally understood what they were trying to teach me.

I had been on a search for happiness, and had finally arrived. I needed nothing more than this moment. My eyes were wide open and my heart was overflowing with love. I was really and truly okay.

I look back at my journey and think there is no way I could have made this up! I bet you, too, can look back and think, "How the heck did I survive?!" But we do. We keep moving. Because our life is a fantastic movie. It's time to start writing a better script so that you can be the fantastic YOU that you were meant to be.

Resources

Each person or organization listed below offers unique wisdom, support, or programs that have been instrumental in my journey, and I suggest them as good starting points for your own growth and development. As I've mentioned throughout this book, you'll find a page of free guided meditations on my website, which is also listed below.

My Websites

Follow Your Joy
www.michele-joy.com

Thrive and Shine! *(this book)*
www.michele-joy.com/thrive-and-shine-book

Guided Meditations
www.michele-joy.com/guided-meditations

Law of Attraction for Happiness Meetup group
www.meetup.com/Law-of-Attraction-for-Life

Authors/Publishers

Brené Brown, *The Gifts of Imperfection*, brenebrown.com

Rhonda Byrne, *The Secret*, www.rhondabyrne.com

Masaru Emoto, hado.com/ihm

Eugene Gendlin, *Focusing*, www.focusing.org/bios/gendlin_bio.html

Elizabeth Gilbert, *Eat, Pray, Love*, www.elizabethgilbert.com/bio

Pam Grout, *E Squared*, pamgrout.com

Louise Hay, www.louisehay.com

Hay House Radio, www.hayhouseradio.com

Hay House Vision Board, www.hayhouse.com/the-hay-house-vision-board-app

Napoleon Hill, *Think and Grow Rich*

Denise Linn, *The Soul Loves the Truth*, www.deniselinn.com

Trish MacGregor, *The 7 Secrets of Synchronicity: Your Guide to Finding Meaning in Coincidences Big and Small*, www.trishjmacgregor.com

Jeff Olson, *The Slight Edge*, slightedge.org

Lissa Rankin, *Mind Over Medicine*, lissarankin.com

Dr. Bernie Siegel, *Love, Medicine, and Miracles*, berniesiegelmd.com

Jean Slatter, *Hiring the Heavens*, creativemystic.com

Neal Donald Walsch, www.nealedonaldwalsch.com

Marianne Williamson, *A Return to Love*, marianne.com

Coaches/Educational Programs

Happiness Coaching with Dr Robert Holden, www.robertholden.org

Tama Kieves, www.tamakieves.com

Soul Coaching with Denise Linn, www.soul-coaching.com

Lisa Nichols, motivatingthemasses.com

Cynthia Occelli, www.cynthiaoccelli.com

Spiritual Teachers

A Course in Miracles, www.acim.org

Abraham-Hicks, www.abraham-hicks.com/lawofattractionsource

Michael Bernard Beckwith, www.michaelbernardbeckwith.com

Dalai Lama, www.dalailama.com

Matt Kahn, www.truedivinenature.com

Matt Kahn, video, *The Way of Radical Acceptance,*
youtu.be/Qh8mZxAkScw

Doreen Virtue, www.angeltherapy.com

Other Resources

Ho'oponopono is the highly respected Hawaiian Forgiveness Prayer. There are countless websites describing the history, development, techniques, and benefits of this prayer, which you can find through a search on the term, but there is no official website.

www.meetup.com
In addition to my Meetup group for the Law of Attraction for Happiness, *Meetup* offers a wonderful way for people to form friendships in person all over the world based on their special interests.

Made in the USA
Columbia, SC
23 August 2018